THE NIGHT SKY

BY THE SAME AUTHOR

Morning
A Letter
Memoir in the Middle of the
Journey
Gabriel Young
Tug-of-War
Hounds of Spring
Happy Endings
Revolution Island
Gentleman's Gentleman
Memories of My Mother
Rules of Life
Cautionary Tales for Women
Hope Cottage
Best Friends
Small Change
Eleanor
The Duchess of Castile
His Christmas Box
Money Matters

The Social Comedy
Evening
Tales of Love and War
Byron's Diary
The Stepmother
The Sodbury Crucifix
Damnation
Games of Chance
The Time Diaries of Julian Fane
According to Robin
Odd Woman Out
A Doctor's Notes
The Fools of God
The Poor Rich
Children in the Dark

The Collected Works of
Julian Fane
Volumes I, II, III, IV & V

The Harlequin Edition

Three Stories of Boyhood
Secrets of the Confessional
A Reader's Choice
A Writer's Life for Me
How to Publish Yourself
A Bad Experience
Mistress of Arts
Can Women Say No?
Ralph's Religion
How to be a Writer
Snobs
The Harrison Archive
In Short

For Children

Meg and the Doodle-Doo

THE NIGHT SKY

A Diary with a Difference

Julian Fane

Book Guild Publishing
Sussex, England

First published in Great Britain in 2010 by
The Book Guild Ltd
Pavilion View
19 New Road
Brighton, BN1 1UF

The Night Sky was written before the international economic
slump, and the author decided not to try to rewrite it with
references to all the financial ups and mainly downs.

Typesetting in Garamond by
Keyboard Services, Luton, Bedfordshire

Printed in Great Britain by
CPI Antony Rowe

A catalogue record for this book is available from
The British Library

ISBN 978 1 84624 442 1

This book of mine and many others are dedicated to my wife Gilly

1

The moon is new this evening, a sickle moon in a cloudless sky, a sweet little silver semicircle in a sky not yet fully black and nocturnal, sharp-edged as if ready to cut through the distance between us.

Days are shrinking. The seasons change, and a change is as good as a holiday; but the passage of time is unchangeable, unstoppable, and more or less unbearable. Strange, how impatient we once were to grow up, we could hardly wait!

A friend of mine was in Highgate Cemetery the other day and had a look at the grandiose memorial bust over the grave of Karl Marx. He reported that fresh flowers were placed on the grave, fresh flowers for the man responsible for the premature and painful deaths of many millions of people and the ruination of ten times as many more. My friend was more pleased to notice the grave of a certain Spencer in close proximity, so Marx and Spencer were not divided by death.

A footnote to history, a political and personal drama, and what will be a period piece by the time this is read, is being played out in the corridors of power and the pages of our newspapers. I refer to the ending of the career of our Prime Minister, Tony Blair. He has governed us for ten years. He gained great popularity and has frittered it away – he grows more unpopular daily. The disaster of his policies becomes clearer for all to see, he is under savage attack from every side, and his face betrays his misery.

Reading Mark Hichens' fine book *Wives of the Kings of England*. He includes Wallis Simpson in his gallery of portraits, although she was only the wife of an ex-king, and by marriage a duchess, the Duchess of Windsor, never a queen. He suggests that King George VI and Queen Elizabeth, later Queen Mother of Queen Elizabeth II, treated the Windsors harshly. King George could have been more generous to his elder brother, and both he and his wife could have been nicer to their sister-in-law, according to the author. But I believe the Windsors were treated correctly. I have reasons to believe so. My parents were friends of the Prince of Wales before he was briefly King Edward VIII. My father and the Prince shared an interest in horses, hunting, point-to-pointing and so on; both rode in races, and both had paid court to my mother. For my father, the last of many straws was that the Prince arrived two hours late at a race meeting of which he, the Prince, was meant to be the presiding VIP. The first races had to be postponed, the crowd was kept waiting, even the horses were upset, and my father, who was the steward in charge, made it known to all and sundry that he disapproved. The point I would make is that my father thought the Prince incorrigibly irresponsible; and his wife and widow, unlovely Wallis, twice divorced, who caused her third husband to renounce a kingdom and an empire, would have continued to do damage to the royal family and the monarchy if she had been allowed to. Queen Elizabeth, wife of the Duke of Windsor's brother, King George VI, blamed Wallis for the premature death of respectively a husband and a father, while Wallis chose to think she and her Duke had been hard done by: how wise of the Court of St James to keep her out of this country!

The resemblances between Edward Prince of Wales/King Edward VIII and Diana Spencer/ Princess of Wales are noteworthy. They equally rattled the royal family for a similar reason: they sacrificed everyone and everything in a search for personal happiness.

My mother never said much about that Prince of Wales. The only fault she found with him was that he was a bit twitchy and kept on straightening his tie.

I met him once. I was introduced to him at Lords Cricket Ground. He referred kindly to my father in a rather laboured voice. He was short of stature, a small person, but dignified. I remember the large knot of his tie, the famous Windsor knot, of course.

He invented the Windsor knot, and a pattern of small squares on worsted material is still known as 'Prince of Wales check'. A gossipy story sums up the pity of his CV: in a nightclub in America, Wallis Windsor told the Duke to 'buzz off, mosquito!' She was interested in another man, she wanted to be with this man and without her husband, and she made a sort of joke in bad taste and revealed an astounding lack of dignity and gratitude. 'Buzz off, mosquito' – what an epitaph!

The Duke's clothes were sold in an auction some years after his death. The jackets looked like cold weather coats for small dogs or chimps.

Exchange in Lewes High Street: an acquaintance asked me, 'Are you still writing?' I answered yes. 'Oh well,' he said in a comforting tone of voice, 'it's something to do.'

This year is the fiftieth anniversary of the publication of my first book, *Morning*, and my fifty years of active authorship. After *Morning* I wrote a short book, *A Letter*, in which I tried to describe the differences between private and public success. *Morning* was a big success compared with my previous five or six years of relative failure, and it made me ill. I began to realise then that my aim and ambition was not to be in the limelight, but to do the work I was called to do as privately as possible. I wanted to tell the truth, the truths of the heart, if through the medium of fiction.

An unintended consequence was that a book called *Verity* took me seven years to write, was never right, and ended up in my wastepaper basket – a fragment survived and has been published. My third book, the one after *Morning* and *A Letter*, was *Memoir in the Middle of the Journey*; and, in literary jargon, while writing it I found the 'voice' in which I could more freely communicate with readers of my books.

Looking back, Lady Luck has favoured me. She has been coy, and on and off quite hostile, but now I realise how indebted I am, and that I cannot thank her enough.

Some rain has fallen after the hot summer, called by alarmists the 'drought'. English governments love extreme weather conditions, they immediately appoint a Minister for Snow or a Minister for Water, and the journalists echo the rousing calls for stiff upper lips, and encourage panic, stocking of food and household necessities, queueing for petrol, and consequential shortages. Anglo-Saxons may keep calm in a crisis, but they adore a drama, which suggests that they lead dull lives. What became of British phlegm?

Memoir in the Middle of the Journey was published

in 1971, and I carried on writing until the publication of *Evening* in 1999. On the last page of *Evening* I emerged from behind the mask of the storyteller and indicated that I had finished with fiction. My impromptu method of telling the tale had become too stressful. Besides, I had no publisher – my publisher had retired. But man proposes ... I was driven back to work. I was lost without it. And I found a new publisher.

Once upon a time I was overjoyed to be a published author. I was an innocent abroad in the Grub Street of middlemen, taken advantage of, not treated well, but I did not know it and did not care. The doors of dreamland had opened and I was at last on the other side. My book was being written about by wise literary critics. People with experience and integrity were approving.

Memories! Memories of long ago!

Today I thank heaven not to be a young writer in this country. Which English publisher is not owned by foreigners? Which English publisher is not governed by the dictates of foreign accountants? Which English publisher will bother to read your book? The fiction called 'literary', meaning more interesting than most, is out, out of fashion, not a moneyspinner. If you somehow get published, you have to face up to the corruption of journalism and the book trade.

But if you have reason to believe our literary scene is exceptionally ghastly, read Balzac's *Lost*

Illusions – the French book industry of the mid-nineteenth century, described probably from personal experience by Balzac, was very like and at least as vile as ours. These days a good book only seems to emerge into the light of day in spite and not because of publishers, newspapers, critics and prizes.

Politics raises its ugly head. People want to be left in peace, the majority do anyway; politicians have other ideas, they are the agents of discontent and worse.

Tony Blair was our Prime Minister thirty-six hours ago. This morning he is only our Prime Minister in name. A handful of his junior ministers resigned their posts in a gesture of rebellion against his leadership, and they have apparently pricked the balloon of his authority.

I cannot love politicians in general. I cannot forget the twentieth century, in which I spent seventy-three years of my life-span. I remember the wars and the blood shed by Mussolini, Lenin and Stalin, Hitler, Mao Tse-Tung, Pol Pot, and the African despots. Also the cruel taxes on living and dying, and that our money confiscated by taxation was seldom spent wisely. Internationally and nationally politicians did more harm than good in that period, and in this twenty-first century I beg them to do better.

A naughty fashion is catching on. More poor

girls are marrying rich husbands and cashing in on the inane divorce laws recently enacted here. The welfare of any children involved is not considered either by the party who grabs the money or by legal accomplices. Nobody can be blamed for anything in our politically correct world. Innocence is guilty and guilt is innocence now, and Alice reigns in the Wonderland of Whitehall.

I witnessed the start of a house catching fire on School Hill in Lewes. I was on one side of the street, immediately opposite was a house under scaffolding – the roof was being repaired, a temporary roof of sheets of corrugated iron covered the area. I first noticed a woman emerging from a house near the scaffolding – she was in a hurry, clutching a baby. She was looking up at the scaffolding, and I looked and saw smoke under the corrugated iron. The smoke thickened rapidly, and a sudden flame curled out. I heard crackling and saw more and bigger bright orange flames. Dramatically a man was running fast down the hill and then climbing the ladder from one level of the scaffolding to the next – he must have been in charge of the repair work and seemed to have remembered something unsafe or possibly illegal. A great commotion ensued. Police constables of both sexes converged on the scene, tapes were stretched across roads, traffic was redirected and jammed, fire engines arrived with sirens blaring, firemen on the pavement were clambering into fire-proof garments, pedestrians were being shooed in different directions, and, as I later heard, the police were organising things pretty well until some apparatchik from the Town Hall gave conflicting orders. I was 'moved on', and after doing my shopping I saw huge cranes with firemen on top holding hoses and aiming jets of water at and into the roof space. Nobody was hurt. The interiors of two or three houses were inundated. I was told that there had been a smaller fire in the same place the week before: which, if true, would suggest carelessness at least. Returning home, I tested my fire alarm.

Many of life's little ironies are reserved for socialists. One of the three aims of the French Revolution of 1789 was 'egalité', therefore the heads of the French King and Queen and assorted toffs were cut off to prove how equal the French people were going to be; yet fifteen years later Napoleon crowned himself Emperor and created a new aristocracy. The Russian Revolution of 1917 shot the Tsar and Tsarina and their children in a cellar to demonstrate that in future Russians would all be workers and comrades; yet not long afterwards Stalin was called the Red Tsar – and he was the most terrible of all the Tsars: which reminds me that I must get down to writing my planned essay, *In Praise of Inequality*.

Hypocrisy is the devil in the detail of socialism. Too much pious hope, pie in the sky, saying one thing and doing another – the human nature of socialists sooner or later, but always, catches them out. That Scottish icon, Donald Dewar, fought against the privatisation of the industries known as utilities, and died leaving a considerable fortune in shares in the utility companies. Socialist politicians conceal wealth in their wives' trust funds; send their children to state schools and have them taught by hired tutors at home; garage their big cars and drive small old ones into their constituencies; keep mistresses in town and wives and children in the country to plug the electoral advantage of a happy family. Blairism is a bad example of socialism in action – a charade, pretence, presumption, affectation. A compassionate society, Blairites boast about, no death penalty here, but they lie in order to lead us into wars that kill the innocent people.

The more we love, the more the object of our love seems to us to be a victim.

From *Dr Zhivago*, Pasternak, B.L.
(1890–1960)

The job of an art critic is to be the judge of beauty, to try to understand beauty in its old and new forms, to redefine and remind us of the highest standards and values, to be down on fakes and frauds, the second-rate and second-hand, and above all to inspire and succour the creators of the beautiful. Yet we have reason today to recall Byron's opinions expressed in his *English Bards and Scotch Reviewers*:

10

As soon seek roses in December, ice in June,
Hope constancy in wind, or corn in chaff,
Believe a woman, or an epitaph,
Or any other thing that's false,
Before you trust in critics.

I recently re-read *Tolstoy as I knew him* by Tatyana Kuzminskaya, the sister of Tolstoy's wife, a book of great interest for a variety of reasons. It was given to me by a generous friend, John McClafferty, thirty or more years ago. It was published in 1948 by the Macmillan Company, New York; translated from the Russian by six named translators; and has an introduction by Ernest J. Simmons, a Tolstoy biographer. In 1973 John McClafferty received a letter from the Manageress of Foreign Rights at Collier-Macmillan International, New York, who was responding to a letter from John, of which I have no record. The Manageress of Foreign Rights wrote: '... this book appears to be quite a mystery. In all of our records I cannot find any mention of the title.' She also referred him to The American Council of Learned Societies – and sure enough a page of the prelims does contain a list of four other Russian books that were translated by the American Council of Learned Societies and published by Macmillan: one was *The Law of the Soviet State*, a slim volume no doubt, written by Andrei Vyshinsky, that gangster who was Stalin's legal henchman.

Tolstoy died in 1910, and Tatyana, his sister-in-law, in 1926. In those sixteen years Tatyana provided and published in parts an intimate and detailed record of Tolstoy, a mine of information for the biographers churning out their post mortems and biogs for ever after. How was it that Americans seem to have had to wait thirty-two years to be able to read a translation of this seminal study of the great writer? And why, so far as I and other students of Tolstoy's life and writings know, did no English translation appear? Why was Constance Garnett translating almost every other Russian text of value of the Tolstoyan period?

But I would hark back to Macmillan: why no piece of paper, entry in a ledger, bank statement, or proud advert, referring to *Tolstoy as I knew him*? There was money in Tolstoy – always has been – why was Macmillan not cashing in? It is hard to believe Macmillan was turning down a commercial opportunity, perhaps to swell the coffers of a Learned Society – Macmillan has never been a registered charity. Moreover, to do the company justice, also the family that created it, philistinism was never their seam of gold. Tatyana's book is delightful as well as informative, a literary achievement, and still enchants nearly a hundred years after it was written.

Anyway, for readers of both relevant works, *War and Peace* and *Tolstoy as I knew him*, a further mystery contributes to the fascination. Tatyana was the model for Natasha Rostov in Tolstoy's book. Her memoir confirms it: she describes experiences of hers that Tolstoy borrowed and transcribed almost as they occurred. He was a writer of originality, created the world of his books, transformed fact by means of his imagination, was a genius, not a photographer; but he was the plagiarist of the life he and his family and friends lived. He held a mirror up to nature with a vengeance. The question therefore arises: did Tolstoy copy Tatyana, or did Tatyana borrow from Tolstoy? Were her own recollections influenced by those of Natasha Rostov? She writes very well, she describes herself and the other people in her book vividly – often her pages seem to be Tolstoyan. She admits in the end that her relationship with Tolstoy was more than friendship and not emotionally platonic. She marries, but feels unable to separate herself from Tolstoy. She is a good woman, but the love between herself and Tolstoy causes her confusion. Were the parts in *War and Peace* about its heroine and Tatyana's memoirs to some extent the same book?

Tatyana Kuzminskaya, née Behrs, must have been exceptional from birth onwards. She had good looks – although she thought her mouth was too big – charm, humour, high spirits, intelligence, and was honest, sincere and faithful – a faithful Christian, too. She sang so well as to be asked to sing at parties, and was mad about dancing. Needless to add that she had sex appeal, and men in the plural were in love with her from when she was twelve or thirteen onwards.

Sage advice to young women of marriageable age: do not marry a man with no back to his head; do not marry a man who loses his temper for any reason while he is courting you; do not marry a man who shows no desire for pre-marital sex; do not marry a poor man by accident; do not marry a man whose breasts are bigger than yours.

There is to be a lunch in London hosted by Book Guild Publishing to celebrate my years of published authorship on 5 October 2006, which will also be Publication Day for my *Odd Woman Out*. I have tried to invite people who have contributed in one way or another to getting my books into print. But social problems arise – who is to sit where ... who can eat what ... how many will actually turn up? – and they put a straw on this camel's back.

My sister June hangs between life and death. She had a hard beginning, since she was born months after her father died, and her end is also being hard. She was a vivid personality, an ugly duckling as a child who grew to be a beauty, charming, intelligent, sympathetic, a social star and a faithful friend. She was also very brave.

As recorded elsewhere, my mother married three times, was widowed thrice by the time she was fifty-five, and lived to be ninety. Her first husband, Percy Wyndham, was killed in 1914, in the war, mere months after marrying her. Her second,

Arthur Capel, was the father of two girls, Anne and June – their marriage was again cut short by his death in a car crash. Her third was my father, they had three children, my brother David, myself and Rose, and he too died prematurely. June was the livewire of our childhood home. She made fun. She married first the distinguished pianist, Franz Osborn, and secondly Jeremy Hutchinson, QC and later life peer. June survives as I write, but I have written of the person she used to be. Her talent for survival was probably the greatest of her gifts, she has lived many more than nine lives and is now in her eighty-seventh year.

Her elder sister Anne died a few years ago. She and June were extremely different. June was intuitive, mercurial, illogical, impractical. Anne knew better, but June with her wit and humour was usually a jump ahead. Anne was pretty but no match for June's looks and appeal. Anne sensed at an early age that she was not so favoured as June, and it had a life-long bad effect. The sisters were always critical of each other, and there was very little love lost between them. Anne had a sadder life than June, but her will-power carried her through, and she was happy with her third husband, Peter Higgins.

My mother's marriage to Arthur Capel was briefer than it might have been. She spent months of her first pregnancy – with Anne – in England, near her sister Laura Lovat and her English doctor, while he remained in France. After Anne's birth she rejoined her husband and was soon pregnant again – with June – and then he crashed his car.

All references to Arthur Capel, nicknamed Boy Capel, require qualification. Recent research has revealed biographical mysteries. He was the son of an English father and a French mother; but he was almost certainly illegitimate. His early years were spent in England, in Brighton, and he went to an English public school; but then in France he inherited wealth and increased it, became a military aide to Prime Minister Clemenceau in the 1914 war, and moved in the highest social circles. He was the sometime lover of Coco Chanel and set her up in her first shop, where she sold hats; but in his will he left a bequest as large as Coco's to another woman. He was a successful industrialist and financier, a serious politician, and the writer of a visionary slim volume; but he is now a posthumous celebrity thanks to the fashionable fame of Chanel, who, after his death, became the mistress of an even richer man, the Duke of Westminster. Romantic gossips have spread rumours that his drive to the south was a flight from his wife, my mother, or in order to keep an assignation with Coco, or was even suicidal because he was missing Coco so badly; but in fact the cause of the crash with a tree was the puncture of one of the tyres of his car. My mother said he could be very charming and amusing, but was occasionally moody and silent. She also said that he tried to recover valuable furniture lent to Coco, that she herself had asked Coco to return it, but without success; nevertheless, she continued to buy hats in Coco's shop. TV interviews of Coco in her old age showed me a tough, clever, busy businesswoman.

At any moment I may become the last living child of my mother's brood of five. And I thought in my youth that I might not live long! I hasten to add that I do not mean to tempt providence with this paragraph.

The Night Sky is a diary without dates, that is the difference.

2

Extremes of behaviour are interesting, at least in principle and to read and think about. They are often the stuff of fiction: normalcy is almost impossible to describe in an entertaining way. Passion, the pains of love, the capabilities of hatred, crime, madness, make a better story than days of toil and slippers by the fire.

Science promises to spot the genes that threaten the health of young persons in later life and somehow eradicate or counteract their potential effects. I understand the health referred to is physical. What about mental health? The gene of mental instability is dangerous and can run through generations of a family.

Owing to over-population and mobility, the services rendered by 'society', by exclusive snobbery, by cliques, settled neighbourhoods and villages, are no longer available. The '400', the top New York families that kept out interlopers, the looser membership of the English Establishment, the Scottish clans, the Trade Unions and the working-mens' clubs, were all repositories of family records. They may still be to some extent; but in their heyday they could encourage boys and girls either to marry or steer clear, to breed or not to do so, they knew forebears, they remembered happy and unhappy marriages, good and bad luck, and especially mistakes.

Knowledge of the history of families is libellous stuff. Each generation acquires it from parents and grandparents by word of mouth and gossip. I have heard tell of mad, arrogant, spendthrift, addictive, unreliable and bad-tempered families – but no names, no pack-drills. Science is not yet offering to reform our genes that cause the most all-round misery. People have to look more carefully than ever before they leap.

The divorce laws in force today seem to entitle one spouse to claim half the fortune of the spouse he or she is splitting up with. However long or short the marriage, and however guilty or innocent the parties to it may be, are not of legal interest. Sex legitimised in church or by law is therefore a sure thing for the poorer partner of a marriage. El Dorado, here we come! Politicians, beware the cost of your divorces which you have sanctioned! Romantics, harden your hearts to the extent of obtaining your partner's signature on a binding pre-marital agreement or a pre-sexual legal document limiting your financial liabilities before you get down to the billing and cooing!

Referring to Pushkin's story, *The Queen of Spades*: he writes it brilliantly, coldly, severely. Its anti-hero, Hermann, hears that an old countess when young gambled and fell into debt, but an admirer saved her from ruin by telling her to play three cards that would win back the money she had lost. Hermann is determined to get hold of the secret of the three cards; his attempt to do so leads to the death of the countess; and her revenge, his punishment, and the moral of the tale is that he wins on two of the three cards and loses all on the third, the queen of spades.

After reading the story I remembered Tchaikovsky's opera, entitled *Pique Dame* in the original Russian version. Tchaikovsky's librettist was his brother Modest, and the brothers between them insert an aria as haunting as the beautiful music. Hermann hides in the countess's bedroom, waiting to beg or force her to reveal her secret. Her maidservants prepare her to spend the night in a chair, and she sings in the French spoken by the educated class in Russia in her era. Here it is:

Ah, que ce monde m'ennuie! Quelle époque! ... Quelles manières! Quelle langage! Ca me dégoûte ... Qui sont les danseuses? Qui chante? Des gamines! Et autrefois, qui danse? Qui chante? Le Duc d'Orléans, le Duc d'Ayen, Duc de Coigny, la Comtesse d'Estrades, la Duchesse de Brancas. Quels noms! Et même quelquefois la Marquise de Pompadour en personne! C'est devant eux que je chantais. Le Duc de la Vallière me félicitait! Une fois, je me souviens, à Chantilly, chez le Prince de

21

Condé, le roi m'a entendue ... Je revois tout comme si c'était hier ... il me dit: je vous aime. Et je sens malgré moi, je sens mon coeur qui bat, qui bat, je ne sais pas pourquoi!'

Forceful advice offered by older women to younger ones should not be followed. Such advice is apt to be perilous. Diana Cooper was noted for her beauty and her bad advice. For example, she made a match between a poor male friend of hers and a girl she thought was an heiress. In fact the girl was a spendthrift without expectations. The consequence was divorce, the only bit of luck was that the marriage was childless.

Margaret Thatcher is the exception to many rules. She gave good advice, she was also a pretty politician. The prettiest women are bored by politics. They are conservative, of course – egalitarianism is not their scene. They are more powerful in their youth than the plain Janes, who take up politics in hopes of asserting themselves.

Our dog Sadie has taken to lying in my study while I write. She leads me into my study after breakfast. She seems to find it peaceful to watch me working.

To visit ill people is problematical. You can be not wanted, can stay too long or too short a time, strike the wrong note, say the wrong thing, make matters worse. You can be too pushy or too diffident. We have heard of a woman who visited her ex-lover on his deathbed and read him the Labour Party manifesto. When I was young I wrote sad letters to a terminally ill friend, but his wife later told me he preferred letters from a socialite retailing the gossip of the town. Friends bring books that weigh a ton or are written by the wrong author to feeble and fastidious patients. My sister Rose never spoke of the cause of her illness and I never broached the subject. I sensed that my brother David did not want to see me much, or for me to see him, after he was so ill, although we were always close. My three visits to June have not done either of us any noticeable good. If possible, I would rather remember my dear ones as they were, in the olden golden days.

Death is not the end. People live on in our memories. I wish I had asked my parents more questions than I did – we all wish that.

We saw *The Queen* yesterday, only the film, that is. The actors do very well. The film is nonetheless a travesty. Our Queen is not like Helen Mirren: no actress could convey the reality of a thousand-year royal lineage, fifty-plus years of monarchy, and a character of great nobility and wisdom. In the film some people get a less fair deal than Her Majesty: Cherie Blair and Alastair Campbell rightly in my opinion. The film-makers are to be congratulated for trying to treat a serious subject seriously, and for reminding the country how irrational and sentimental it was about the death of the Princess of Wales. Incidentally, the mother of Queen Elizabeth II was nothing like the actress who was chosen to act the part.

Monarchy is one of the great mysteries, also one of the evergreen topics of conversation. To kill a king is not a good idea – witness the fairly modern experience of England, France and Russia. Greek literature, Roman history, Shakespeare's plays, would support my discouraging view. Vienna strikes me as a sad city with its fine 'royal' buildings now used for common or garden purposes. Spain recalled its royal family with resounding success, just as we did in the seventeenth century. Predictably most politicians are against the recreation of a role that would rob them of the chance of becoming the president of a country. The power of monarchy is where the mystery begins. Monarchs are easy to kill, but their murder is difficult to live with. There is a sort of 'holiness' in kingship which cannot be laughed to scorn by atheists, revolutionaries, by the crude dogma of Cromwell or Marx or Lady Macbeth. Solzhenitsyn has often warned post-Marxist Russia that it would be in trouble for not being penitent or showing contrition for its regicide, oppression and bloodshedding. Now Russia denigrates Solzhenitsyn and would deny his record of the horrors of the USSR, the Union of Soviet Socialist Republics.

*   *   *

At my age, in my dotage maybe, I feel enabled to ask an awkward question for the umpteenth time: what became of the accomplices of the tyrants of the last century, their secret policemen, torturers, executioners, the staff of the Lubyanka Prison, the staff of the Gulags and the death camps, the African butchers, the homicidal Asians? Some of the top men have been caught; but the underlings who mass-produced the fears, the screams and the death rattles, how did they escape, how could they live with the memories of their cruelty? And there is a present tense to my question. What on earth do the merchants of misery and mayhem think they are doing for their self-styled gods, for their wicked paymasters?

The woman that deliberates is lost.

From *CATO*, Joseph Addison
(1672–1713)

On the twenty-seventh day of this month of September, 2006, my half-sister June died. The experience of having been the brother, close friend and beneficiary of June for nearly eighty years cannot be described and summed up in one note amongst others.

The Labour Party's annual conference, Tony Blair's last, has ended. On the final day there was a speech by John Prescott, the Deputy Prime Minister; there had previously been speeches by the Chancellor of the Exchequer and the Prime

Minister. They shared a common denominator: they were all farcical. The Chancellor, Gordon Brown, was accused of lying by Cherie Blair, the PM's wife; the PM told us his many failures were actually successes; and John Prescott apologised half-heartedly for having damaged the country, abused his position, humiliated his wife, and made us all look as foolish as he is. Shame on the electorate! Democracy that handed over great countries to the Bolsheviks, to the Fascists, to the Nazis, has yet another reason to blush and hang its head.

Not long ago we were treated to the celebration of the centenary of the birth of John Betjeman. It was like a curtain-raiser to the Labour Party Conference in as much as it released a tidal wave of misrepresentation and misapprehension. The fact that so much of John's literary output is mockery seems to have gone way over the heads of even the majority of his admirers. His humour is a sophisticated version of that favourite resource of humorists – laughing at the parlourmaid or, to put it bluntly, a 'class' lower than one's own. Take his most famous poem, 'Phone for the fish-knives, Norman': it is a collation of words that are considered non-U by people who think themselves U – I refer to Nancy Mitford's booklet, *U and Non-U*, her guide to the lingo of the toffs of her era. John is caricaturing and satirising the linguistic pretensions, euphemisms and affectations of certain upwardly mobile middle-class persons. For examples: 'phone' is meant to be a common abbreviation, 'fish knives' are frowned on by society hostesses, and 'Norman' is an unfashionable Christian name. The poem is clever and funny if you happen to catch its full meaning, but it is now taught in state schools. Most people must love it/buy it for the wrong reasons. Again, we were told by several of the fans singing John's praises that he was a lover of the suburbia he wrote and made films about. What he also loved was to ridicule the suburbs in his original and charming way. He once drove me to look at the house where Evelyn Waugh was brought up. He was not paying homage or visiting a shrine: because Evelyn Waugh had begun to impersonate an eighteenth-century squire, lived in a stately home, wore loud check suits and drank too much port, John was making a joke of his relatively humble beginnings. His jokes were always good if you could see them, but are surely caviar to the general. I am his fan, too – I value his friendship and was very fond of him – and would if I could rectify the public perception that he was a cosy amiable old buffer and a 'people's poet'. He was no more the 'people's' anything than the late Princess of Wales was the 'people's' Princess. She was an aristocrat with a lineage as long as your arm. John in later life moved in the highest social circle.

If John Betjeman benefited from being mistaken for a 'people's poet', Tony Blair benefited from good old British snobbery – he was mistaken for an English gentleman.

What has he done for us? What has he done to us? Thanks to Blair's 'open frontier', we will be crowded out by immigrants and can expect revolt and even revolution. Scotland, encouraged by Blair, will try to break the Union with England – Scotland and Wales could become independent little countries, like Andorra. Inflation caused by Blair's overspending is probable. The laws of the land, muddled up by Blair, will not be able to maintain order; and state schools and hospitals, owing to Blair's maladministration, will be shunned by responsible parents and ill people who are not attracted to unruliness or fever pits. The better news is that, according to our scientists, we shall soon sink under the seas of climate change.

Shall we turn the page? My new book, *A Doctor's Notes*, is due to be published in a few days. It will be my thirty-first, not counting fifteen 'little' books, the Harlequin Edition. Frustrated writers might like to know that my literary career grew out of dissatisfaction and dejection. Half a century ago a family friend staying with my mother reminded me of my childhood. She passed a remark intended to comfort me for not getting anywhere with my writing. 'You always have a happy childhood to remember,' she said. Well, I did remember it, and the story became my first book.

There are writers and writers, some cannot help doing it, others regard it as a job and hope it will be a meal ticket. I plead guilty to belonging in the former group, therefore the story of my life consists mainly of sitting down and committing millions of words to paper. Not quite a thriller! Balzac apologised for his detachment and absent-mindedness thus: 'A writer is always thinking of the next chapter.' Thomas Hardy was so wrapped up in his work that his second wife complained. 'You have not spoken to me for weeks, you have not uttered a word,' she said. He contradicted her: 'I have.' 'When was that?' she inquired. 'This morning,' he replied. 'Who did you speak to?' 'The milkman.' 'What did you say?' 'Good morning.' Evelyn Waugh wrote *Brideshead Revisited* in a room in a small hotel far enough from his family and home: he wanted not to be distracted. The lives of these writers were not nearly so dramatic as the tales they told. It could be claimed that the more intense, emotional and gripping a book the quieter must have been the life of the author while writing it: witness Emily Brontë cooped up in her father's vicarage and producing *Wuthering Heights*. Some writers, however vocational, are not prolific: Manzoni spent almost the whole of his life writing *I Promessi Sposi*. Others take time off between books, Turgenev, for example. But they are all writing nonetheless, look at their volumes of letters. David Cecil often remarked that his biographies of writers were uphill work, and expressed a hope that nobody would ever attempt to write his biog: certainly, it would have been a pity for him to become less entertaining dead than he was when alive. In my youth a friend of my literary leanings advised me to travel round the world in order to garner copy for the stories I might write later on. I did not follow his advice. If I had I might have been another of the authors of action-packed bestsellers.

My stroll down memory lane is inclined to be bookish. *Morning* received lots of reviews – it was easier to get a review fifty years ago. The majority were kind, but one critic loathed my book. The hostile criticism rankled for years, although I hesitate to claim that the pain of being blamed surpassed the pleasure of being praised. In due course the same critic gave a book of my short stories a rave review. Much later on, when my Collected Works was published, I put a quote from the rave review on the back of the jackets of the five volumes. There was a launch party for the Collected Works, and I invited the critic to it. The invitation was refused, but I received a letter of apology for the bad review of *Morning*, which had been reread and enjoyed.

What is the etiquette? I did not write to thank for reviews when I started out. Now I do, for better or worse. Critics need to be encouraged, too.

Being a writer of many books is no big deal. Writers make things, like engineers, architects, carpenters. Art exists, but where does craft end and art begin? Inspiration can be traced to love, hate, vitality, illness, neurosis, and the surge of energy that precedes an epileptic fit, as in the case of Dostoevski. Pride in a finished article is mixed up with relief that it is no longer your business. Good feelings, if any, are soon swamped by regrets. You are haunted by afterthoughts. You remember mistakes that were never corrected. A couple of silly words are like the drumbeats at an execution: too late, too late! You could do it all better if you had the chance. Time is the only eraser of such negative notions. Your book becomes a sort of dead letter, ancient history, while the future beckons seductively – another project is germinating in the hothouse of the imagination.

Which of my books do I like best? The last one, of course. Which do I most dislike? Sorry, I don't want to put ideas into the heads of those who would do me down.

Odious comparisons: men with white beards all look alike, so do men with unshorn black beards, and even with black moustaches. Small men are drawn towards big cars, flamboyant attire and tall women. Tall men fancy small women. Female invalids always carry a handbag, although it contains only a tissue and they badly need both hands for walking sticks and other aids to balance. Fashion is infectious: young women suddenly dress alike internationally. Children are slaves of fashion. Certain hair styles obliterate identity. A living skull without hair is bad luck, the hairless skulls of athletes and fashionable men are bad taste.

Do I revise my work before publication? Ad nauseam. My first revision is almost a rewrite. Further corrective readings by myself, my copy editor, and the printer's proof reader, amount to five or six. One error in the finished article usually slips through the net – pardonable nowadays maybe, but would not have been allowed in the good old days. Other writers' attitudes to revision are interesting. L.P. Hartley gave his MSS to his typist and never looked at them again. Ursula Codrington, who typed for Leslie Hartley and me amongst others, revealed that Leslie left spaces in his MSS for her to fill in with adjectives. Van der Post, author of *Cry, The Beloved Country*, apparently handed his MSS over to his wife and let her do as she pleased with them. Computers have had huge effects on the work of authors, not always good.

Computers are a closed book to me, but ignorance is usually ready to voice an opinion. I write with 2B pencils and delete by means of a rubber, my manuscript is then transferred by my typist on to a computerised version, which facilitates corrections and the movement of text. I forget the names of my characters as the story goes along, the maid in chapter one called Dolly becomes Miriam in the middle and Ethel in the end; computers enable you to be consistent. I do not write long and learned tomes, but occasionally I read them or try to. If such modern books are packed with astonishing detail, they betray the computer responsible. Gibbon's *Decline and Fall of the Roman Empire* made him famous not least because he knew so much, had so many names and dates at his fingertips, and was almost inhumanly in control of his material; we no longer marvel at books as heavy as his one. Yet these advantages of computers are increasingly questionable. They make many books too long judging by human capability and established standards of art. They confuse us with their feats of memory, which make our heads spin. Above all, they lack the personal touch. What may be ideal for factual books is bad for fiction, the sort of fiction that is essentially emotional. The hand of the author has not shaped his story by holding the pen or pencil that touches the paper. Photographs are not paintings: they are mechanical: computers are also machines. Artists are made of flesh and blood and souls, and the mysterious inexplicable ineluctable truth is that art, literary and otherwise, is a communication between souls. Materialists and atheists, scoff if you will! I shall quote Wordsworth: 'the dry product of the scoffer's pen'.

In the brave new world of today – or is it the cowardly new world? – nobody can fail, we all have to win the prizes, and the idea of anyone being better than anyone else is taboo. Cowardly or crazy? But I grit my teeth and scribble the dangerous words: some writers are better than others. I dare to be more heretical and risk being burned alive by the Inquisition of liberal do-gooders: better writers are more interesting than bad ones, clever people than dunces, and the dramas enacted in palaces than the fates associated with the kitchen sink.

How strange! I satirise egalitarians and levellers, the dumbing-down of school exams, the lowering of standards of politeness, respect, behaviour, dress, honesty and morality, while the popular programmes on TV are all about cut-throat competition.

Let me re-state the obvious: we are more fascinated by leaders than losers, by those who have stayed on top for generations, also the shooting stars, persons climbing up the greasy pole, the best people and the ones who succeed in being better, the rich, the great. I would suggest that in my line of work the energy required to fuel the work of getting there is produced by tension. It was William Blake who told an aspiring artist: 'You fear everything, so you'll do.' You are a perfectionist or you are nothing, and the fear of failure and unreasonable angst drive the perfectionist towards the goal that is always out of reach. The physical and mental effects of the strain of doing good work explains the writers' blocks, mysterious ailments, desperate remedies, and casualties along the road to Mount Olympus. The other obstacle is social life in the widest sense. The pram in the hall is the cross of the artist. As for high jinks, they are the end of high art. Unwary artists have been hunted and brought to bay by hostesses.

More metaphors descriptive of the tribulations of writers occur to me. Getting ready to write is like cranking the engine of a car, or pushing a car downhill to start the engine. After 'unwinding' on holiday, the writer has to be wound up. A break from work seldom recharges his engine, he is more likely to lose the thread of his work. On a night out with non-literary friends he will probably drown his book as well as his sorrows. In literary company he will talk away his book. Flattery in higher society will tempt him to amuse by betraying all his secrets.

I wrote *Morning* on a 'low', I published it on a 'high', I reacted to the 'high' by sinking 'lower' than ever; then I 'lost' several books by letting people see unfinished parts of them and listening to unhelpful opinions.

3

A young writer protests: 'Are we to be the monks of literature? Are we to eat bread and water in hermitages? You paint a bleak picture of our destinies!' I reply: 'My picture is one of three. It's a triptych, and I've painted the panel on the left, descriptive of your apprenticeship. Now turn to the panel on the right, which you will find even bleaker. For you and I live in a philistine country. I can't say whether it is more or less philistine than other countries, all I can say is that it is more philistine than it was when I was young.'

Some years ago the top publishing houses, and leading publishers in a financial sense, were allowed by politicians and influential bodies to abolish the Retail Price Maintenance Agreement. This meant that there was no fixed price for books, publishers and booksellers could sell a book for any price they could get. But it meant more than that: cut-price books were not merely an idealistic liberal notion, they flooded the market, quantity took over from quality, fully independent booksellers could not afford to compete with the bargain basements of chain stores, bookshops selling better books lost their living and had to close, making it well-nigh impossible for the writers of non-bestsellers to market their work. Greed won, liberals had sold the pass as usual, and now greed rules the industry. Exceptions are exceptional. Standards are lowered repeatedly to appeal to the masses.

And what sells today? What do publishers push by means of hype and bribery? Mainly non-fiction, apparently. The glory of English literature was always its imaginative work, poetry and novels; but I seldom see full-size reviews in newspapers of high-class fiction. The unwritten law for literary editors is not to venture over the heads of the most limited readers of the newspapers that employ them: nothing that might be unpopular is allowed. Bad grammar is not to be mentioned. Good prose must not be praised. Middle-brows reign in so-called posh papers, and the tabloids cater for the lowest brows.

So how do you get into print? Can you afford to?

The central panel of the triptych answers a different question. My first step on the slippery slope of being hooked on writing was the discovery that I could read. Unforgettably, I found myself reading a proper book, *Mr Midshipman Ready,* by Marryatt. The experience was like love at first sight between monogamists.

In time, I realised that an English sentence could make sense either in a humdrum way or could have grace, wit, personality. A great sentence differs from the New English Bible, written by a committee. Compare the best writing with writing that is merely grammatical. Strain to hear and to recognise either discords or sweet harmony. For writers who persist come what may, the addictive element is beauty. It, or she, is elusive, we never can lay a hand on her, she is poised on our horizons, and she remains the breath of our lives. The sculptor Henry Moore said that he always waited to see whether or not an aspiring artist could do good work at the age of fifty-five. Well, I have joined the band of octogenarian writers, and still seek the thrill of one day creating something beautiful. Young writers, the lesson you must learn is a hard one, for the ultimate prizes are unworldly and unwinnable; but my long life dedicated to beauty does not seem to me to have been wasted.

Ailing person speaks to an acquaintance who happens to be a doctor: 'I know how busy you are, everybody wants your advice, but I wonder if you'd let me come and talk to you briefly – my GP doesn't fill me with confidence.' Doctor replies: 'Of course, no problem, my patients are all dead.'

Language is a Russian doll. You say or write something, then feel the need to qualify it, define, clarify, defend or change it: you reject the first layer of doll and expose the next doll and the one after that. And so it goes on until you are reduced to wondering if animals are better at communicating than we humans are.

I wonder if my imaginary idealist can afford to be a writer. Ignoramuses may believe that a literary type writes a good enough book without undue difficulty, sends it to a publisher who sees its merit, a contract is signed and sealed, critics review the book in newspapers justly and with benevolence, and the writer and publisher live happily ever after on sales, reprints, film rights and translations into foreign lingos. Optimists have some catching up to do.

To begin with, forget fairy stories, think of blood, sweat and tears. 'Publisher' is not a synonym for 'aesthete'. Publishers who love books are extremely rare, publishers who read books are uncommon. Most publishers are dependent on the books they publish – they need money in order to feed themselves and their families, they are businessmen and will look at books submitted for judgment as if with the eye of the pawnbroker, guessing its value, its worth, and what they would be able to sell it for. If a publisher, usually the last of many to whom the book has been submitted, offers a contract, more than likely the author will have to pay in one form or another to get into print, up front by a contribution to the costs of production, or by not receiving any royalty until sales have covered those costs, or by jiggery-pokery over rights, or in some other roundabout way. Will the book be a bestseller? By chance, maybe; but ordinarily not unless it is hyped. Top authors expect to have a quarter of a million or half a million pounds for advertising included in their contracts for a book. Will yours be reviewed? Do you have friends who are journalists? Do you know many critics? Will your book be on show in the shop windows of booksellers? Yes, if you pay for the space.

And what happens if you do not have the money to pay the bill for becoming a literary figure? Nothing much, it could be said. You did not expect the world of literature and art to be a street market. You were not prepared for horse-trading and monetary horse-play. You are a poor scribe, and will have to wait and hope that Lady Luck favours you before you are forced to earn a crust elsewhere, in some industry less like a casino, where less money is on the table and more integrity.

There is one other answer to all these questions. It may be a true answer, but never has been or will be proved statistically. Optimism asserts that talent always rises to take its rightful place in the hierarchical firmament.

What is philistine about our nation? More to the point, what is not? The Church of England is responsible for the New English Bible; our government deceives us, wastes our money, wages wars and commits homicide in a big way; our judiciary is outmanoeuvred by an Egyptian shopkeeper; our fourth estate, the press, is largely owned by foreigners; film stars and footballers are our oracles; and our united kingdom is disunited.

Remember! A novel called *Dr Zhivago* by Pasternak rocked the monolithic USSR, and another novel, *One Day in the Life of Ivan Ivanovich* by Solzhenitsyn, brought the communist Russian empire crashing down. Another novel, *Animal Farm* by George Orwell, put a final nail in the coffin of twentieth-century socialism. What is mightier than the sword is the pen of novelists, of writers with the deepest imaginations and the most courage; yet in Philistia, our native land, novels of all sorts are bundled together and treated like dirt.

Look again in the catalogues of the sales of 'art'! The most expensive items could well have been 'painted' by decorators, jesters, mental cases, children, or are dreamed up by ingenious photographers. Study the 'architecture' of the Scottish Assembly's buildings that cost England so dear. Go to 'conceptual' productions of operas.

Not prejudice, valid comparisons.

Philistines rule, OK?

Listen! There never was an artistic period.
There never was an Art-loving nation.

from *Ten o'clock*, James McNeill Whistler
(1834–1903)

Dear optimists, did you think I was exaggerating when I wrote about the bribery and corruption of the book trade? On the 18th of June 2007,

The Times printed the contents of a letter from Waterstone's owner to more than three hundred of his bookstores nationwide. The letter sets out what he can do for books and the costs of doing it. Top price is £45,000 – no, not a joke – for £45,000 one book will appear in his shop windows on to the street, be on display in the front of his stores, feature in Waterstone's national press and TV advertisement campaigns. No more than six books can receive the £45,000 treatment. The price for hyping books goes down in steps, to £25,000, £17,000, £7,000 and £500. The alternative to not buying Waterstone's endorsement of a book is not pleasant. An order of 1,000 books can be cut to 20. So endeth the lesson! Anyway, Waterstone's customers who did not read *The Times* on a certain day in June will think the books they have bought must be good because they were recommended by Waterstone's staff.

A postscript to the gnashing of my teeth about the abolition of the Retail Price Agreement governing the sale of books. In Lewes, my home town, the effect was that three modern bookshops closed. They could no longer compete with a stationery chainstore that sells books at about two thirds of the prices printed on the dust jackets, the prices that gave them a living. I had begged the Royal Society of Literature to campaign against a measure so harmful of good writing, good publishers, good booksellers; but Roy Jenkins, head of the RSL, wrote a typical politician's letter refusing to help. Recently, I received a letter from the RSL, urging me to support small independent bookshops. I wrote back that the Society's change of mind was not better late than never, it was too late.

Laugh and be well.

The Spleen, Matthew Green (1696–1737)

Well, yes: revolutionaries are the clowns of the politics show, if you forget their victims. Lenin was yelling 'kill kill kill' until he was knocked out by a stroke. Stalin was Russia's version of the Red Queen in *Alice in Wonderland*: her cry 'Off with his head' was always good for a laugh. Hitler was understudying the part of *The Great Dictator* in Charlie Chaplin's funny film. Chairman Mao might have been beaten every day and twice on Saturdays by his horrible wife. The African tyrants have amused us by eating their enemies.

What has the farce of modern history achieved? Oliver Cromwell beheaded one king and ushered in another. The French regicides lasted less long, Napoleon crowned himself chop-chop. The Bolsheviks took seventy years to wreck Russia, but they made a good job of it. China is closing the gap between left and right by saying they are the same thing.

Politics has its leitmotifs. The pen is funnier than the sword in this context. The more meaningless the words of politicians the worse it is for the rest of us. What did, and does, communism mean – mass murder, an alibi? What does capitalist mean – somebody with savings? Where do the 'masses' begin and end? Who is middle class, who is higher than the people in the middle? Define 'bourgeois' in clear English prose! Define that cliché of today's politic-speak, the 'hard-working' man, the 'hard-working' father of a family: is that man, that father, a member of a trade union run by bosses who are trying to get him to work less hard, or is he self-employed and works twice as hard as the unionists, or is he a member of the Rothschild family who work night and day to make money? Can you answer these questions? I bet you cannot. Yet they are the articles of faith of millions, of billions, the credos, what is believed in, worshipped, suffered and died for. They are the toys of the apes of God.

Idealism does not feature in the paragraphs above. But here is another question: how and when does idealism turn into hypocrisy? Hypocrisy is more common than idealism by miles. Hypocrisy is the besetting sin of a great many of the politicians and their supporters who have strutted their stuff in my lifetime.

Yes, I refer to communism and its fellow-travellers, socialism, the Left, levellers, the rich who pretend to be poor, the slummers and the dressers-down. Karl Marx read Dickens to his children, *Great Expectations* and *David Copperfield* no doubt, the endings of which books are happy because the heroes become capitalists. Comrade Lenin was the white hope of international idealism or utopianism, of liberal intellectuals, sentimentalists, discontents, and the vengeful brigade. But after he had his stroke, he was pictured in his palace surrounded by expensive nurses; and the greatest of atheists was then embalmed and displayed in a glass case, idol-fashion, to generations of the masses. It had been written in the Marxist version of a bible that religion was 'the opium of the people', a drug to keep them quiet peddled by capitalism; yet Lenin himself became a patently false god, lying in his glass case and half-made of wax, still daring the masses to protest, hypocrisy personified. And the phony 'kings' of other communist states imitated Lenin, reigning by means of terror and murder, and writing their booklets of maxims in letters of blood.

I am old and free, at least free to speak my mind, and write it – every age has compensations. I could never vote for a politician who refuses to believe that everyman wants to be more equal than others.

Here is a pithy criticism of the political type written by Charlotte Perkins Stetson Gilman (1880–1935):

> Cried all, 'Before such things can come,
> 'You idiotic child,
> 'You must alter Human Nature.'
> And they all sat back and smiled.

Charlotte Gilman, of whom I know nothing except two quotations, also wrote:

> I do not want to be a fly!
> I want to be a woman!

Gordon Brown is our new Prime Minister, and we all have to wish him luck: partly because he seems not to be a lucky man. Here's hoping he does not govern us unluckily! As Chancellor of the Exchequer he sold our gold cheap, and he is unelected. He was not chosen democratically to be our leader. I fear for him, and for us. But enough said!

Wonderful W.S. Gilbert (1834–1911), provides me with a good thought for the day:

> Politics we bar,
> They are not our bent;
> On the whole we are
> Not intelligent.

Some political people rage at me for belittling and blaming their colleagues in my books. I know that many politicians work beyond the call of duty and serve their electors honestly. My generalisations have firm foundations nonetheless. I was born in 1927, only a few years after my two uncles were killed in wars. Their father, my grandfather, died a sadder man than he would have been if his sons, even if one of them, had been spared. My mother sorely missed her two brothers, and a husband, another casualty of the 1914 war. My own brother, served in the 1939 war with distinction and was wounded. In the two great wars members of my family lost innumerable relations and close friends, not to speak of the losses of health and careers. Meanwhile, away from the home front, the Russian revolution of 1917 was setting out on its homicidal spree, which would kill tens of millions of Russian citizens by internal repression. Hitler followed where Lenin led and murdered at least six million in his holocaust. Then came the 1939 war, accounting for still more millions of dead people. And the grand total of victims has to be added to, even doubled by, lethal activities in the Far East and the Middle East. This modern bloodbath, unparalleled in history, has all happened in my lifetime and is the bright idea, the achievement, crime and shame of politicians. No wonder I warn my readers how dangerous they are.

I report gloomily that our new Prime Minister spoke in Downing Street before entering number 10 – boredom ensued. Look forward to lumpy porridge from now on!

Gratiano in Shakespeare's *Merchant of Venice* says: 'I am Sir Oracle, and when I ope my lips let no dog bark!' Shakespeare is mocking self-styled oracles, who get everything wrong. All the same I venture to be oracular, for no one will take any notice, and if by chance notice should be taken I will not be around to realise how wrong I have been. My oracular prophesy is that Brown's premiership will end worse than it has begun.

Moreover I guess that the wreckers' lanterns and signals are guiding our ship of state onto the rocks.

4

My long book, *Cautionary Tales for Women*, was too short.

Why should we be friends with so many young women whose husbands have left them unexpectedly, minus any means of support, and with little children to look after?

Women are said to love a rotter. An amusing criminal is pardoned by the fair sex. Of course, they cannot be too pernickerty – many of us would not be where we are, alive and more or less kicking, if our mothers had reserved themselves for perfect men. They have to be hail-fellow-well-met, and simultaneously as sharp as a needle and as perceptive as a sniffer dog – that is, a bitch, a canine one. Sex can be camouflage. Sex covers a multitude of sins. Youth with its imperious urges likewise. But sex, and for that matter love, are not everything for everyone. There are hints and signs that women fail to see, understand, take seriously, at their peril. Some horses have a wicked eye, some animals are untrustworthy, and men may have that look which spells trouble, that attitude which jars. Money, for instance, can mean more than a kiss. Money is the commonest passion for which men commit their crimes. And the crimes against women are classless and uncountable. Look into those eyes pleading for your favours, ladies, and flee if you should detect the star-like glimmer of avarice, envy, a secret agenda, a gambler's determination to throw the dice one more time whatever the costs and whoever will have to pick up the bill.

The husbands of my aforesaid friends gambled with their own money and other people's, with family funds, lost the lot, and were prepared to let their wives and children starve.

Those wives are nice, decent, well-brought-up, and not fools. They were amazed that men they willingly married, whose children they had borne, could be so bad. Desertion was the least of their problems. One husband used a joint credit card to incur debts of fifteen thousand pounds for which she was responsible, he had gone bankrupt. Another husband, who had also opted for bankruptcy, caused bailiffs to arrive at the family home without warning and take away the sitting-room furniture. Both wives tried in vain to contact their husbands, who had both lost jobs – nor were their mobiles working. In the end the wives swallowed their pride and applied to in-laws: but a mother-in-law sided with a son, a sister-in-law with a brother, and neither would give any information, let alone assistance. They engaged solicitors at fees-per-hour they could not pay. Divorce proceedings were set in train, but the solicitors warned that they were not charities, and that no money was likely to be obtainable from bankrupt spouses. The wives were defeated by the appetites of their children, and eventually sought Welfare handouts.

Although relations and friends mounted rescue operations, the stories did not get much happier short-term. The children were millstones as well as reasons for living. The wives suspected their husbands were cheating over bankruptcy too, were actually gainfully employed, and comfortably installed in West End addresses. Financial support was only coughed up under pressure, money towards the rent of a cottage into which one wife had removed, money to help to pay the school fees of the children of the other wife. The emotional blows were equally devastating. The wives had obliged their husbands, the husbands had said they were satisfied; but the wives cried while the husbands seemed to be laughing with other women.

These are extreme cases. They are made worse by being middle class. Poor people are more accustomed to hardship. Rich people have the benefit of money. But in all skirmishes in the immemorial war of the sexes there are winners and losers. It is bad news for every loser to be mistaken, to have been fooled, to be rejected, and sad to be unloved and lonely. In short, the experience is horrid and hurtful, and the apportionment of blame is a futile exercise.

Girls, beware! Be prepared! Study men and money before flower arrangement. Gamblers ruined my friends, and gamblers are not the worst sort of men to give your hearts to.

If you think I exaggerate, think again! Several of the finest estates in Britain, belonging to families for generations, properties acquired by talent and merit, were lost by gambling in the last few decades. The owners of the stately homes were more or less ruined, if only relatively – some were still richer than most people. But the ruination of the poorer classes, of punters at race meetings, in casinos and betting shops, is not relative, it sinks gamblers and their spouses and dependents to the bottom of the financial sea.

Women are my hobby-horse – no offence intended. I mean I love to study them, and have actually published some of my findings. Even at my age I feel inclined to shake my head over them, lecture, scold and rap their knuckles for their own good. I beg their pardon, but cannot promise to stop.

Admittedly, no generation is in favour of chaste postponement. We – myself and my male contemporaries, fairly polite youths from law-abiding homes – ground our teeth and bewailed the fact that for us it was all talk and no do. The boys and girls of today – our grandchildren possibly – may pity our inhibitions, our capitulation to conventions that were still almost Victorian, our agreements to hold back, take no for an answer, be careful and not ruin anybody's reputation. Yet the truth of the matter is that the relations of the sexes have never been a bed of roses, and the descendants of Adam and Eve have always found disadvantages as well as advantages in the rules and regulations that govern their mating.

And after all we had our fickle flirting, eye contacts, scented letters, hands held in secret, a dance that was like a rehearsal, and invasive kisses lasting a long long time.

Dear youth! My aunt, my mother's sister, Barbara Wilson, née Lister, wrote a highly praised book with that title, *Dear Youth*, and here I am writing that my youth was also dear.

We wanted to be older. We were more conscious of what we did not have than of what we had. We hungered for love or sex, and did not know the difference. We were taking wrong turnings, smashing into dead ends, losing our bearings. Our loves were mostly made in hell, not heaven. Mistakes were our staple diet. Feelings were always being mutually hurt. Yet, looking back, I see one picture superimposed on another, a study in sunshine, all of us laughing, and nearly blotting out the second picture of the same people in the shadows of destiny.

The symptom of love is when self-centredness becomes aware of concern for another person. Happiness is benevolent, we can afford to be kinder than we were. Since we suffer if she suffers, and vice versa, we start to understand the bargain we have struck. We acknowledge and respect the rules of tradition – we do not want the loved one to break rules about fidelity, reliability, honesty, and cleanliness. We are caught in the spider's web of dependence, we discover the strength of the silken cord, we fear the possibility that she or he might not always be there for us, beside us, supporting us, and are more careful not to set a bad example.

Does the tale have a happy ending? It has a happy beginning. Girls on pedestals never fall in love with gamblers, nor do they dally with married persons in difficulties, or sadists, or bullies, or drug addicts, or flirts, or bores, or spendthrifts, or impotent men, or misers, or spoilsports. But pedestals crumble, and girls turn into women and wives; and I am too truthful a writer of fiction to suggest that my heroines live happily ever after.

Negative tales are easier to tell than positive ones. At my age I have a preference for ease, and am willing to record objectively the passions by means of which the human race comes to grief.

What is supposed to be good for young women nowadays is not good for everyone. The suffragettes got what they wanted, as women do, but their votes have not been markedly beneficial to their sex, let alone to mine. All of us have mothers, and we live to notice that women do some things better than men. But – to pursue the generalisation – they have not turned warlike men into peacemakers; they have imitated men instead of reforming them; with one exception they have not shone in our Parliament.

No one is to blame for anything, according to the liberal philosophy. I disagree – I lived through most of the last century. Men are to blame for Marxism, communism, socialism in action. Men can seem to be too stupid to reign over us: only dimwits could have believed that communism would or could change the spots of the human race. But women, beloved women, why did you fail to restrain them?

Sorry, I have another question: why do you follow the fashions wherever they lead? Fatherless babies are denied a human right. And babies grow up and may not forgive you for thinking they were better off without a daddy.

Yes, you can have abortions, but which sex gains most from them? And who is risking the post-operative trauma, possible future infertility, lifelong regrets?

Yes, you have the pill, but its convenience is questionable. It weakens the argument of refusal, makes it more difficult for a girl to say no, encourages men to behave even more selfishly.

Yes, you have divorce laws, which can help you to escape from disagreeable marriages, but also mean you will ruin or be ruined by your ex.

Jack and Jill got married. He was a librarian,

she was a model, they were ill-assorted – he was twenty years older than she was, she had more get-up-and-go – but they seemed to rub along. Jill had to be in France for a photographic shoot, fell in love with a Frenchman, abandoned Jack, and vanished. Several years passed. Jack traced her, she was living alone in a Parisian suburb, pleaded with her to come home, promised to forgive her, tried to mend their marriage. She repeated that it was all over, she had never loved him and never wanted to hear from him again. He had discovered that her Frenchman was a Roman catholic, married with eight children, and had given Jill the push; but she would not return to Jack. More years passed, and she rang him up. She wanted a divorce – she would not say why – she had instructed a solicitor to do the necessary. As a result, Jack had to sell his house and hand over half the proceeds, also give her half of the money he had saved. She took every penny she could get, and all the jewellery that had once belonged to his mother. He was broken-hearted, nearly broke too, and could not forget that she had only let him make love to her once.

Maud was the only child of rich people. Her father was dead, her mother was ailing, and she was in her late thirties, a plain heavily-built spinster. Mother and daughter decided to take a cruise in the Mediterranean. On board the ship Maud was ogled and pestered by a small dark fellow-traveller, an Englishman with Spanish blood, called Arturo. Late one evening, after she had put her mother to bed, she stepped out on deck for a breath of air. Arturo was there and spoke to her as no man ever had before. It was not gentlemanly, he harped on her virginity, and described his sexual preferences and proficiency. She should not have listened to him, and definitely should not have arranged to meet him on the next night. The consequences were two hours of savage copulation in his cabin; his proposal of marriage and her acceptance in the small hours; breaking the news to her mother, who suffered a seizure; a wedding conducted by the captain of the ship; and a homecoming which included Maud's mother's removal in a private ambulance to a nursing home. Three children were born, while Arturo took care of her money. He got her to sign papers in return for satisfying her sexual appetite. She had been well-off before her mother's death, she was very rich afterwards. Not long after the funeral Arturo threatened to sue for divorce. She was devastated. His first monetary move was to claim the profits he said he had made by speculating with her money: she owed him six of her eleven million pounds. She paid up in hopes of reconciliation. She then learned from her solicitor that he was divorcing her after all and seeking a fifty-fifty split of her estate. He issued a sworn statement, denying that he had already received six millions of her money, and asserting that he could no longer put up with her fantasies and lies. The authorities chose to believe him; he made off with more of her money. She tried to look on the bright side – Arturo had done her many favours; but her solicitor reminded her that she and her children were going to be not far from destitute, and she cried on his shoulder after paying his great big note of fee.

Two other women, more lamb- than mutton-like, were led to the slaughter and will serve as examples. Judged in a court of natural law, their men were wrongdoers, exclusively greedy and mean, unprincipled, irresponsible, and without a glimmer of conscience; but they pretended to be gentlemen. They thought they were better than oiks. They were pretentious snobs. One had a doting mother who played bridge and told her son he was good however bad he had been. The other mother was fiercely competitive and determined to prove her son could be more successful than his father. One of the two, Patrick, was plump and had a job in an estate agency – he dreamed of becoming rich by fair or foul means. Number two, James, was an idle rascal – he was an interior decorator.

Nicky and Vicky, the mistresses of Patrick and James, had only done what lots of other girls of all classes were doing. They took the pill and slept around. They were pleased to shock their parents. They had fun, sort of. Nicky fell for Patrick and Vicky for James: actually they fell into bed with their respective boyfriends, it was more lust than love, the matchmaker was availability. And sex was habit-forming and put the idea into the girls' heads that co-habitation would save a lot of trouble. Patrick agreed to move into Nicky's flat, it would be a good deal for him. Vicky had private money, and James persuaded her to rent an expensive house for him to live in. Then Nicky forgot to take the pill and a child was born; and Vicky got maternal, sought fertility treatment, and she and James were blessed with another. The consequences were more or less brutal messages left overnight on kitchen tables.

The girls could not believe their eyes – they were unaccustomed to reading. Nicky thought the note was meant for the milkman, Vicky thought James had gone somewhere on business. Reality dawned on them slowly and typically. It began with confusion. They had been cooperative, why were Patrick and James not cooperating? They had been almost like wives, why were Patrick and James not behaving like husbands and fathers? They had thought they were happy, they had assumed that everything was OK. Perhaps they had been selfish, and switched their attentions from lords and masters to babies; but they had trodden the customary path of motherhood. They blamed outside influences, matriarchs, other women, tarts, bribery. Anyway, they were wounded deeply, unable to cope on their own, in financial difficulties, frightened and lonely. The ultimate question was: why had they been singled out for wretchedness stretching into the future?

Tactful friends were soon supplying answers. It was bad luck, hard cheese, the fault of men, of two men in particular, a shame for the children, an all round disaster.

Some boor mentioned red lights. A spoilsport said you are supposed to stop at red lights. Then a puritan saw fit to preach that modern morals were to blame, liberalism that laughed at respectability, lawlessness that was more admired than tried and tested conventions - in short, modish feminism, which had played the part of the Judas goat.

Nicky and Vicky's defence was more basic. They had done nothing wrong. The had 'kept up' and 'gone with the flow', and were not ashamed of being in favour of 'freedom'. Sex had been fun, and they could not help it that making a baby was as easy as falling off a log.

5

Unfortunately, some would say, this is – or, they hope, was – the age of permissiveness.

Male writers for donkey's years have nagged women not to be miserly with the favours they can do for men. We have also had two great wars, and wars are heydays for sex, voluntary and involuntary. Then trends were set by tactile actors in Hollywood and elsewhere, by dopey pop stars, porn kings, thick-headed athletes, tabloid journalism, and addictive substances. The top thing to be doing was promiscuity. So men got what they had wanted, and, typically, changed their minds. They did not think much of willing women. If she, whoever she is, woman in the street, partner, was doing a man's job and behaving as lustfully as men, she could no longer count on chivalry or proposals of marriage.

Patrick did not have to wait to have his way with Nicky, and James was soon satisfied in the bed of Vicky. Both couples gravitated in a hurry from being 'boyfriends' and 'girlfriends' to 'going out together': a euphemism if ever there was one. Babies came along for both, and the runaway train of events crashed, causing casualties.

A hackneyed tale, an everyday story of happy-go-lucky folk, of accidents waiting to happen, no doubt; but a 'but' presents itself. Although Patrick and James were exemplars of male chauvinism, they were not violent rapists, they were not even rapists. The girls had the chance to protect and preserve their virtue. They could have said no instead of yes. They could have resisted temptation, decided not to 'adapt' so readily to men they scarcely knew, and restrained their feminine inclinations to be seduced by compliments, to repay them, to be kind and have pity. They were not clever girls, their little brains had been washed by all the feminist propaganda. They acted on impulse, 'freely', as they had been told to by H.G. Wells, D.H. Lawrence, psychologists, pulp fiction, films, and sex-educationalists.

Did they ever love their technical lovers? They thought they did. They assumed that what they made separately in the prologue of their stories was love, not a mere physical response comparable with the blowing of a nose. Every chapter was really about ignorance, thoughtlessness, careless-ness, an offence against happiness, for which the punishment was bound to fit.

I think the more interesting part of the story, the appendices, if you like, is twofold.

Here is appendix one: without blaming my heroines,

without objecting to the spirit of the age they were living in, and without suggesting that any other age and the sexual culture thereof was superior, I would draw attention to the profligacy of Nicky and Vicky, their wastefulness. In olden times, the wisdom of mothers and grandmothers was to teach female descendants that they were launching into the wider world with at least one treasure, a means to a good end, a jewel of perhaps inestimable price, their virginity – or, failing that, the less valuable but not worthless access into their bodies. The wiseacres pointed out that men would desire their youth, their beauty, and they would and could reciprocate, but what were they going to get out of doing so, except babies and drudgery? Love is a bargain, they said, and love that is not is hot air. Do not sell yourself cheap, they said, abstain, be sensible, confer your treasure on the highest bidder, and win a better life for yourself and your children. Nicky, Vicky, a percentage of their contemporaries, and younger girls, either never received such advice, or came from homes in which it would be considered disgustingly materialistic, or have got the wrong ideas from the wrong schools and influential sources, or are simply too bold or frivolous to care; and they suffer accordingly. Women no longer young, with children and debts and divorces and troublesome exes, will not easily find another man to shoulder the burden they have become. Teenage mothers with buckshee babies are not what every man is looking for. Their mistakes cost more and more. The best thing mothers can do is to warn their little girls: 'Don't be like me, don't be fools, act in the interests of your kids, seek the chance of living happily ever after!'

Appendix two refers to the sort of people Nicky and Vicky were. Nicky was a 'sweet girl', as the saying goes. Her father had been a soldier, but perished young in a minor war, and her mother brought her up as well as she could, to go to church on Christmas Day, clean her teeth, be polite and try to pass her exams. She was an only child, and she and her mother were close until a stepfather came between them and puberty put its spoke in their wheels. She made new friends, racy rebellious teenagers, and went with them to work and live in London, and do as they did. She lost her virginity and had a series of one-night stands. Patrick was different. His difference was that he wanted her more than once. He paid her physical compliments, he bought her with his flattery. She was his doormat, he commandeered her dignity, will power and self. She made allowances for him, overlooked his vulgarity, thanked him for siring their child, Mark, and was grateful for his maltreatment.

Patrick spoke to Nicky on the telephone some days after he had left the note on the kitchen table.

She wailed on hearing his voice: 'Oh Patrick, Patrick, where are you? What's happened? What have I done wrong? Patrick, please tell me!'

'I've told you to mind your own business.

Didn't you read my message? You're not to bother my mother – she doesn't know anything anyway – we're finished, Nicky, kaput, and that's my last word, understand?'

'But Patrick, how can you? Have you forgotten Mark?'

'Mark's not my business, he was your accident on purpose.'

'Oh no, no, that's too cruel, honestly. I've given you all of myself...'

'Well, I'm giving it back to you. I don't want it or you. It's a clean cut, see, and that's final.'

'But we've no money, you can't let me starve.'

'You've no right to my money – I never made promises – your people can take the strain. Bye-bye, Nicky.'

'What about your clothes?'

'I'll send somebody to collect them.'

He rang off.

Vicky was as active as Nicky was passive, but both were fools of fashion. Vicky donated her virginity to an older man at a summer dance in the country – it happened out of doors, in undergrowth, and was quick and businesslike. She scarcely knew him, had danced with him a couple of times, was excited by the intimacy of his style on the dance floor, and let him finish the job. She experienced little pain and no physical pleasure. On the other hand she had been ashamed of her virginity, was impatient to be a member of the smart crowd, and had started taking the contraceptive pill. She got what she had wanted emotionally. She never knew the name of the man and never saw him again.

Nicky and Vicky were not acquainted. They had something in common nonetheless, along with the myriads of other females dating back to Eve. They were girls at risk in different ways, Nicky owing to her ignorance, Vicky because she thought she knew it all.

James, Vicky's so-called 'young man', had one of those bad reputations that bait a trap for women. His would-be victims called him 'Byronic', his real victims called him 'devil'. He had boyish good looks, wavy hair, and wore tinted spectacles that concealed his eyes, and his intentions. Vicky and he were aware of each other as soon as she latched on to his set or clique. She too had sex appeal. Her features were aquiline, she looked fierce, 'like a Red Indian', somebody said, but when she laughed or giggled her face crumpled in a disarming way.

They had a teasing relationship to start with. She meant not to fall for him as all the other girls seemed to do. But at a party he annoyed her by flirting with an old hag, then he drank too much, she supported him back to his flat, put him to bed, and agreed to climb in beside him. She had spent odd nights with a variety of men. None of her affairs had amounted to much. She liked to play the field. She assured herself that a spot of fun with James was neither here nor there.

He never thanked her for looking after him. He was a cooler customer than she was. He ignored her. And he got her goat. She succumbed to the extent of wooing him rather than the other way round. When he asked her to do his shopping, she complied, delivered the foodstuffs to his flat, cooked it, and again shared his bed. He conquered her by taking her for granted; but she believed it was the other way round, that she was the top dog who let him gnaw some of her bones. She performed other services for James to try to squeeze a word or two of appreciation out of him. She knew he was behaving badly and she was being rather rash, but she was driven on by the knowledge that he would find another girl to spoil him if she refused – she swallowed her pride inch by inch. She took up residence in his flat and he sacked his daily lady. She valeted his suits and cooked and cleaned. They frequented restaurants less often, he invited his friends in to meals, and sometimes she was not allowed to join his male guests she had cooked for. And by mistake she got pregnant – he was such an impulsive lover – and with twins.

She had not thought about marriage. She and her set regarded matrimony as history, and not the answer. But she could not hold down her job as receptionist in a five-star hotel when she was pregnant, she would be hard-up, she had no savings – what would become of her babies and herself? She had never asked James for anything except cash to buy their food: he had done the asking. To play the part of a weak woman in the family way was against her principles and dragged her idea of her independence in the dust. At the same time she was fired by recollections of her menial service and the overdue payment she deserved. She was owed a gold ring on her finger, or some sort of financial assistance, or at least a clarification of her position. She worked up quite a hatred of her James, who was not hers, and was at last prepared to cross-question him.

It was at breakfast time – she could not bear to wait any longer.

'James,' she said.

He did not raise his eyes from his newspaper.

'James,' she repeated between an order and a wheedle, 'what surname are our twins to have?'

'Oh God!' he grunted.

'I'd like them to have your name.'

'Is that so?'

'You're their father.'

'Am I?'

'Stop it, James! Stop reading that paper! All right – listen – can the twins have your name?'

'What are you driving at, dear?'

Vicky's anger took over.

'Can I, James? Am I ever going to have it? I'm not feeling well, and you take everything and give nothing in return. I've been good to you, and now you're not being good to me.'

'Are you by any chance speaking of marriage?'

'No, not when you put it like that, but I'm

sick of your selfishness, and now I've your children to consider whether or not you do.'

'I see. You're proposing to me. Well, I'm not accepting your proposal. I'm turning you down. I thought you were against marriage. You're not the girl I knew. And I don't know you, Vicky. And I've got a hangover, so please change the subject.'

She cried.

He continued: 'One baby would be bad news, twins are beyond the pale. There it is! This evening – dinner – I'll be bringing back a couple of mates – seven o'clockish, make sure we won't run out of booze.'

He duly deserted her. He left the note on the kitchen table on the day after she brought the twins home. His message was more curt than Patrick's: it was, 'Sorry, dear.' He kept an appointment in New York, and never came back. She tried to sell his house, but it was only rented. She was lucky to get a council flat in a slummy area because of being a single mother with the two kids.

Some would say that Nicky and Vicky were exceptions to the rule of the countless girls having a high old time with a minimum of red tape; but, since I with a small circle of acquaintances have encountered two casualties of liberal propaganda, both in dire straits, they cannot be very exceptional.

Even if a thoroughly modern miss is happy to shrug off the chance nature has given her to pause for thought before she welcomes a man into her body and perhaps her soul, a moral tale is still worth telling: ask the doctors doing abortions, the divorce lawyers, and the children of divorcees.

I am not an Utopian. Sex is not for pausing. Sex is not wise, and sex has no conscience. But girls make babies, and the temperament of mothers differs from the temperament of fathers whatever the feminists claim, and the old real rule is that women without foresight are apt to get clobbered.

Nicky and Vicky were bad pickers. They picked so badly that, in order not to come to grief as quickly as they did, they should have either judged by common sense and etiquette or asked for guidance by means of a brief questionnaire: 'Is he polite? ... Is he kind? ... Is he not beastly? ... Is he not mean?' The fathers of their children could not have given the right answers to those questions.

Nicky's Mark was soon eight years old, and was ceasing to be her recompense for the pains of producing him. He was no longer her very good boy, faultless in her eyes, for she was no longer his beloved mother who could do no wrong. A third party was to blame. Patrick had chosen to twist the knife in Nicky's wounds. He drove into the mother and son's lives in his red soft-top sports car and drove off with the boy.

Nothing was the same for Nicky. The 'same' looked much better in retrospect than it had at the time. She knew it on that first day, when Mark came home with his armful of manly presents, a baseball bat, boots on wheels, a fishing rod, live maggots, and a book about making bombs. Even she could see that she had been superseded in her son's affections. Mark could talk of nothing and no one else. His hero-worship was hard to listen to. Patrick's absences made Mark's heart grow fonder, he pined for his father in between the few hours of occasional visits.

Nicky would have compared herself to an animal caught in a trapper's noose, if she had had a comparative turn of mind. She tried to protect herself, but movement in any direction tightened the noose. She had not been pleased to see Patrick again, but she was immediately under his thumb as before. She protested against his marching into her home and stealing Mark, and he made a public issue of it.

'Your mother wants to have you all to herself, Mark. You heard her, she'd like me to get lost and never set eyes on you again. You tell her what you think of that!'

She had to cave in. She had to pretend to be glad that Mark had found his father. She had to take care not to voice any criticism of Patrick which would provoke defensive anger and abuse from Mark. She was permanently in the dock these days, for Mark did not forgive her for having split up with Patrick.

'But it wasn't my fault,' she said on one occasion.

'He told me it was.'

'But that's not true!'

'Father doesn't tell lies.'

'You don't know him well, Mark – you don't know what you're talking about.'

'Why are you nasty to him?'

'Me? Nasty? You don't know the half of it. And you mustn't be horrible to me. We were friends before your father waded in.'

'He's my friend now.'

'Oh Mark!'

The son bore resemblances to his sire. He was as hostile to Nicky as Patrick had been. She had dreaded educational developments, that Mark might win a scholarship to a boarding school somewhere and she would be deprived of his company; now she began to hope for such a release from his scowls and bad temper.

Her private life might improve if Mark were elsewhere, at school, or, better still, living with his father wherever his father lived. Nicky had formed a tentative relationship with another man, Leonard, a schoolteacher; but she had not dared to expose Leonard to her difficulties at home. She made excuses for keeping Leonard and Mark apart, she was offending Leonard for fear of Mark spilling beans to Patrick, who would not miss a chance to be unkind. She had no personal conversations with Patrick since he began to see Mark, but at last her feelings of despair forced her to speak to him.

One weekend day he was picking up Mark,

and she called him back into the entrance passage of her house.

'What is it?' he asked irritably.

She began to tremble, but managed to say: 'I don't like what you're doing to Mark.'

'He's been mollycoddled too long, he needs a father.'

'Not one like you – coming out of the blue – keeping the boy on tenterhooks – always waiting for you – and then to be spoilt with expensive presents. Why not take him to be with you for a few months at a time?'

'Oh no, none of that – my partner wouldn't say thank you.'

'I didn't know you had a partner. I know nothing. You shouldn't come here in that swanky car – we're all poor people. You make difficulties for Mark.'

'Stow it, Nicky! You're not entitled to know, understand? I'll abide by my laws and do exactly as I please.'

'You've ruined my life.'

'More fool you!'

Nicky and Vicky could have said 'snap!' to each other, if their paths had crossed.

Vicky was tougher than Nicky. She put a brave face on having been deserted by James. She was not going to let that despicable brat wreck anything. She looked around for another man to fill the void, and found one or two; but they were the short-stay kind. The worst of all the problems for Vicky as for Nicky, unforeseen and insoluble, was the relationships of the children with their respective fathers.

Vicky's twins were called Janet and June, not christened. They were harmless babies, attractive toddlers, and loved by their mother in her unconventional slipshod way. They survived moveable bedtimes, unpunctual meals, food past its sell-by date, and made a good impression on strangers. But Vicky's lovers were not paternal types willing and able to care for another man's children. Little Janet and June also had an adverse effect on Vicky's search for a job – she could only work part-time, and part-time pay did not keep the wolf from the door of the flat in the remote suburb she was reduced to living in.

She had to swallow her middle-class principles of pride and beg for government charity. Her slapdash methods with money plunged her into debt nonetheless, and under pressure she revealed her plight to her parents.

It was a come-down, she had sneered at her respectable father and mother, who both worked in the offices of the NHS. She was a prodigal daughter, but no fatted calf was killed to celebrate her return. She was scolded non-stop, her twins were turned into sticks to beat her with: poor fatherless babes being dragged up by a scatty and selfish mother. She should have done the right things – look where the wrong things had landed her!

But these difficulties were eclipsed by another. The twins were close friends, wrapped up in each other, as somebody said, and aged five, six and onwards exclusively so, it seemed. Vicky began to feel she was shut out of their secret preoccupations. She could not always under-stand their twitterings, and was no longer sure whether or when they were listening to her or paying attention. Then they asked questions about James.

He was their father, it was natural, or could have been, but it surprised and had an unsettling effect on Vicky.

What is he like? they asked almost in unison.

'Oh, I don't know, I haven't seen him for ages.'

What was he like?

'Pretty helpless.'

Weren't you helping him?

'I tried to.'

Why did he go away?

'Largely because of you two.'

Why?

'He wasn't a lover of children. He had to be the one getting looked after.'

Did he say goodbye to us?

'He left in such a hurry, I don't think he said goodbye to anyone.'

Did he say goodbye to us while we were asleep?

'Not that I know of, I don't think so.'

Did you know he was going?

'I did not. He left a note.'

What was it?

'I'm not saying – it wasn't nice.'

Have you got the note?

'No – but I wouldn't show it to you anyway.'

Why not?

'Because it was awful, and I don't want you to think too badly of your father.'

Janet looked at June, and June said: 'He wouldn't be awful to us.'

Similar interrogations occurred, and there was an element of ambush. The twins seemed to wait until their mother was unprepared and more or less unable to defend herself, for instance when she was cooking or talking on the telephone.

One of them would say: 'Could we go and find Daddy?'

The other might raise her voice and repeat another question: 'We want to search for him on the internet – help us, Mummy, help us!'

Then they asked for a photograph of James.

Vicky had been dismissive of the twins' interest in their father; and annoyed; but she was hurt by it, and felt somehow threatened. She had liked to think she was a free agent, and the extraordinary idea crossed her mind that she was besieged by hostile forces.

'I haven't got a photograph,' she replied sharply.

Janet said: 'Please look in your desk.' And June actually rummaged amongst Vicky's luggage stored at the back of a cupboard.

That June found one made matters worse. Both twins were triumphant, and rubbed it in that their mother was careless, uncaring, and trying to stop them loving their father because she had hated him.

Vicky denied it.

'I'm not standing for all this nonsense. Your

father left me for no good reason, he was the cruel one. I've sacrificed a lot for you, and I won't be continually put in the wrong. You're most ungrateful, and if you're not careful I'll have you adopted.'

The twins giggled. The next thing was that they wanted an extra copy of the photo and two frames. They kept the framed photographs on their bedside tables, and Vicky suspected that they addressed their prayers to James.

There was a fourth actor in the drama engulfing Vicky. She had a lover, Malcolm Brown. After James' departure, she was determined not to be minus a man in her life. Malcolm was the manager of the local branch of a banking group, a bachelor, not very romantic until Vicky taught him a few tricks, and at first a temporary solution from her point of view. They met on two or occasionally three evenings a week, he would come to supper and to fulfil his lover-like duties, and did not dawdle afterwards as he was set on getting a full night's sleep. But Malcolm was dependable, a quality not to be despised by the person Vicky was turning into, and for the years that passed she was too preoccupied to seek a replacement.

In the amazing situation of being bullied by her twins in their early girlhood, Vicky's opinion of Malcolm underwent a change. She talked to him more seriously than usual in the course of one of their assignations, after supper when he was replete, and before consummation, when he would be keen to reach agreement and get down to it.

'Malcolm,' she said, 'we've been together quite a long time, I've grown to admire you and love you more and more, and I'm lonely without you and wonder if we could unify our lives in one way or another. I'm a much steadier woman than I used to be, and would promise to be nice to you and make you comfortable and happy.'

He disappointed her. He did not jump at the offer. His response was cautious to the point of unyielding.

'What form of unification do you mean?' he inquired.

'Well – that's really up to you – it's not a leap year.'

'I can't propose marriage, Vicky.'

'May I ask...'

'I think not...'

'But you owe me an explanation.'

'Vicky, your children...'

'Oh my children! They need help so badly, they'd be good if an authoritative person was in charge.'

'Judging by what you've told me many times, they're obsessed with their father, your previous lover.'

'Oh but that's a crush, they'll grow out of it.'

'I have to say no, Vicky, for the first and last time.'

'Malcolm, don't desert me!'

'But you must see –'

'No, I don't, and I'm sorry too, but I have to tell you I'm not just new skirt.'

'I appreciate that, and hope we can carry on as before.'

'No.'

'Pardon?'

'You heard me.'

'But Vicky...'

'I'll fetch your coat.'

'This is unnecessary.'

'Not unnecessary for me. Go away, Malcolm.'

'Vicky...'

'Don't touch me! Go!'

'What a pity!'

'You can say that again.'

He took his coat and his leave, and she cried as never before, not boldly, not with dignity and not with hope, crying for her waste of time, crying for having had to eat her hat, crying so much that she woke the twins, who stole downstairs and stood looking at her silently.

Will Nicky and Vicky ever find true love? Love for a woman counts for much more than fornication, the vote, the right to do men's work, careers and worldly success. That is a truism, a platitude, but none the worse for that.

6

Today the sun shines after weeks of English summer weather and flooding. Aerial photographs suggest that the flooded areas are mainly where – as socialists would put it – 'affordable houses for hard-working families' have been built, in other words on the outskirts of old towns and often on designated 'flood plains' set aside in the past to absorb excessive rainwater.

Polite society is polite because it does not drop bricks or tread on other people's toes. Here are a few sentences that should not be spoken in polite society or anywhere else for that matter:

1 'You are looking tired/ill.'
2 'I can see whose son/daughter you are.'
3 'Will you do me an enormous favour…'
4 'Thanks for your novel, I'll read it as soon as I've finished the absolutely fascinating book I'm reading at present.'
5 'Thanks for showing me round – I'll tell you who's got a really beautiful house/garden.'
6 'Can I ask your daily lady to do a little work for me?'

7 'I'm afraid I'm not hungry and you've cooked all this food.'

8 'I'm asking you to my party although you won't know a soul.'

9 'Why on earth is your son/daughter so clever?'

10 'You're lucky – to be having an operation for a heart bypass/liver transplant.'

Modern Love in sound bites:

'Fine, thanks, but sometimes a bit lonely...'
'He's nice, but married, of course...'
'He's not happy, she's no good...'
'What would happen to him if I didn't...?'
'I like adventure, I'm the impulsive type...'
'Why should three of us be unhappy...?'
'I must, for his sake...'
'She never cared for him, she's asked for it...'
'We'll have a blessing in church...'
'I know I'm lucky, but...'
'He won't ever take no for an answer...'
'I forgot, and was caught napping...'
'She's a sweet baby, but I'm not ready...'
'He's rushing me again...'
'I told him to get it elsewhere...'
'He's going with a girl, I'm really angry...'
'She's a tart, a gold-digger...'
'I gave him everything, that was my mistake...'
'You can't say no to a man like him...'
'Now he's asking for a divorce, the rotter...'

'He'll pay a lot more this time...'
'All that money's not for me, it's for Baby...'
'Not bad for three years on a bed of roses
– well, bed, anyway.'

Vow, a noun, formerly unbreakable promise,
lifelong commitment, now usage confined to
archaic texts and humour.

Tony Blair has become a Roman Catholic. He
previously went through the motions of being a
Protestant. Has he become a peacemaker? He
was a warmonger, and his war is still being
waged.

Turncoats are hard to trust; but, according to
Francis Bacon, writing in *On Atheism*: 'A little
philosophy inclineth a man's mind to atheism,
but depths in philosophy bringest men's minds
about to religion.'

Banks all over the world have been greedy and
are having to eat humble pie. Their shareholders
are on slimming diets.

Recession is the buzz word; economic immigrants
work harder than we have been doing for less
pay; job wars, car wars, water wars are all on
the cards; lights are going out; the government
has alienated Islam; our government is as bad as
the weather; my end may be nigh.

But half a year has passed and it is already

springtime. The rooks are nesting, and I have heard blackbirds tuning up for the summer singsong. Life is sweeter than ever, and luck that is not bad is the more appreciated. Good deeds still illuminate the little corners. I write against the odds, in spite of anno domini, national calamity, widespread unemployment, bankruptcy, hardship, need, and because it would seem ungrateful to carp and whine when I personally have reasons to cry in an undertone 'halleluia'. Writing was always my escape and liberation. I am happy to write however sorry I may be. This book, if it is ever finished, will be my fiftieth, depending on how you count.

Above is not to say I will not point a finger at folly.

We could have a last laugh at that old booby, Karl Marx. He was entitled to dream his dreams, but not to mislead people with their dreaminess and plunge humanity into years of suffering. Marx did not even know that animal nature is competitive – why was he trying to write a 'better' book? Had he never looked at the birds and beasts, been in the country, gone to a zoo, had dealings with children, deduced anything from the evidence all around him? Socialism–communism only works by means of fear, oppression, the crushing of the innate call to aspire, to have hopes and to yearn to realise them. Marx peddled the promise that he would make the poor rich. For God's sake, Russia, admit you were fooled! You won next to nothing, you lost more than you won, and you led the dance of death worldwide. Time to bury that mummy in Red Square!

He made false promises, he tempted the hungry and thirsty, and gave wickedness its chance. Marxist dictatorships did not 'wither away': Lenin died in the lap of luxury, and Stalin because his servants were too frightened of him to open his bedroom door.

In *The Decline and Fall of the Roman Empire*, Edward Gibbon observes: 'History ... is, indeed, little more than the register of the crimes, follies, and misfortunes of mankind'; but Gibbon did not squeamishly avert his eyes from those crimes and misfortunes, far from it, he recorded them as suffered by the Romans in full and ominously. Perhaps the old are duty bound to have a shot at telling it as it was and is, and not worry too much about being shot at by the big boys with their critical guns – or do I mean the little boys with their big guns?

My harsh opinion is that liberals promote what they are against. The twentieth century was bedevilled by liberal counter-productivity. Lenin and Hitler were opportunists, and won power by creating circumstances, rigging elections, cashing in, largely because liberals were the pigs in the middle, piously hoping, dithering and do-gooding, and ham-stringing the opposition.

Rereading *The Passions of the French Romantics* by Francis Gribble, an old book, a surely unobtainable book, and a fascinating one. It was published by Chapman and Hall, and the publishers did not provide a date of publication. The 'romantics' in the book, whose names might ring bells for English readers, are Lamartine, Alfred de Vigny, Alfred de Musset, George Sand, Victor Hugo, Alexandre Dumas, Prosper Mérrimée. They made love in their fashions in the early nineteenth century, and their loves were the inspiration and/or the subject of their writings. They were not 'gentlemen' whatever their breeding, their trade was to kiss and tell: George Sand was not a 'gentleman' in any sense, for she chose a masculine *nom de plume* and dressed rather like a man, she was neither a gent nor a 'lady', for she too washed her dirty linen in public and for gain. Sex was not always the object of the exercise, although several of the objects of love were courtesans. Some of the girls were actresses, who put up with literary lovers in hopes of having a play written for them to perform. George Sand urged young girls to do as she had done, and 'follow nature boldly', which in the context meant 'be promiscuous, unfaithful, selfish, tough', advice devised by a plain woman in need of reassurance.

The English climate encourages pessimism and promotes melancholy. I believe syphilis was called the English disease in France. The English disease today is depression. When I asked a lady from the Philippines if her people suffered from depression she did not understand me. I had to explain the symptoms. She said she had never heard of an illness like that. But she knew a lot about drink.

Victor Hugo features in the book about the French romantics. He is enough to put you off romanticism for life – a liar, a faker, a go-getter without scruples, a cruel sentimentalist, a pompous buffoon, whose main achievements seem to have been to subjugate and suborn the journalists. Some of his books have made good films and at least one musical, but does that equate with literary glory?

People have told me for sixty years that I wrote the wrong books. I have been told to write ripping yarns and become a paperback, or my autobiography inclusive of scandalous revelations, or film scripts, or the wording of adverts. A relation urged me to write more children's books like my *Meg and the Doodle-Doo*, and less of the 'serious stuff'. I have been asked to write biographies: 'You'll do better with a biog.' Well, the book I am collecting material for will be called *The Philistines of England*, and there will be room in it for the advice I have received. And I might follow that volume up with another, called *The Sexual Secrets of High Society in my Lifetime*, which should earn enough money to cover my funeral expenses.

We are off on holiday in a few days, to the

South of France, God willing, same hotel, same room in same hotel, and when we return I shall probably have to have a surgical operation.

7

A word more, if I may, ladies, actually a paragraph or two if you would not object, a word of advice, which I mean to be kindly avuncular and hope you will not think bossily chauvinistic.

Our young girls today dress either to kill or be killed – no, I am not joking. Bare legs, very short skirts and no bras are not the right kit for pub crawling, and consequences range from rape to murder. Jeans with holes in strategic places also ask for trouble. And the absence of a panty-line visible under a tight skirt or trousers is the opposite of modest. Who on earth encourages or allows girls to take such risks? Have the mothers, and probably the teachers, had so little sexual experience? For heterosexual youths a more or less pretty girl is one big erotic zone. I know the most available girls are not the prettiest; but those who undercut prostitutes only get the type of men who look least desirable in the sober light of day.

The girls in the paragraph above, who play with fire, may well grow into the sex-starved middle aged women still dressing unwisely. They do not disguise the weight they have put on, squeeze themselves into trousers, and forget that the average man does not fancy an excess of flesh. They show off wobbly arms and wrinkled cleavage. They wear lipstick that could be blood. Have they forgotten, or did they never know, that sex is a performance much more complex for men than for women, and that lovers of a certain age have to be cajoled, excited gently, not scared stiff? They should conceal their more ample charms, dress with reassuring dignity, and learn to stimulate by means of the aphrodisiac called sympathy.

Vita Sackville-West, otherwise Lady Nicolson, was like Lady Chatterley and her gamekeeper Mellors rolled into one.

Back at home – no operation yet – at home and at work, and very nice too, although our holiday was good. Yes, back on our poor little funny old island – but why kick a country when it is down? Our friends in the sunny South of France are charming, although they spoke well of Tony Blair and even thought Gordon Brown was not a bad Prime Minister.

Back in time to see the government adding to its collection of pets. The additions are a pair of serial murderers, the Ipswich strangler and the bus stop murderer, and another murderer who cut a young girl in pieces in order to rape her. The pet-loving politicians, with the approval of do-gooders, will now keep the homicidal trio caged up in prison for decades or until they die.

They will not see their pets, they would rather not see them, they only want to be sure they are out of harm's way, unable to do any more harm privately or politically, and being cared for in considerable comfort notwithstanding the swingeing cost to the taxpayers. These politicians are probably a tiny minority, the merciful minority who have no wish to make the punishment fit the crime, and are proud to boast that they are against the death penalty. They reserve their killing for the innocent civilians of other countries, the thousands and tens of thousands of blameless men, women and children they kill and maim in their unrighteous wars.

With apologies to the great W.S. Gilbert I would slightly amend the refrain of his song for the international Establishment:

> Common sense we bar
> It is not our bent;
> On the whole we are
> Not intelligent.

Yes, yes, but some of us, despite our lack of intelligence, know that politicians can cause grief. We have to look back at what they have done in order to guess at what they will do next. We need to study to survive. Politics always has been and remains the second most interesting subject to preoccupy persons of sensibility. The first subject is, after all, religion. Both are scary since they are in charge of our destiny.

Eighty-odd years on this planet tempt me to provide chapter and verse of the folly of my race. I have a powerful inclination to throw stones from within my glass house. The foolishness of Adam and Eve has been dealt with elsewhere. I think of more modern times, and its comedians who have kept the generations in fits. Let me remind you of their catchphrases: 'Man was born free, and is everywhere in chains ... Liberté, Egalité, Fraternité ... The dictatorship of the proletariat.' Pause for laughter, while we try to count, or to estimate, the billions of people who were killed for those absurd phrases. Revolution is the most popular of all shows for the groundlings, the brainless masses. But not to get too serious – who cares about the folk of yesteryear who fell for men calling themselves Jacobites, Marxists, Fascists and Nazis?

The joke of my reading of fairly modern history is the gullibility of people. Those who believed in panaceas, pie in the sky, and that all was for the best in the best of all possible worlds, should have worn the cap and bells. Loud laughter is reserved for the silly-billies who guillotined Queen Marie Antoinette and shot the last Tsar of Russia and his family. Humour is cruel, we laugh in order not to have to cry. We can split our sides by remembering those French men and women, those clever tasteful proud French people, taking the politics of liberty, equality and fraternity seriously. Liberty is a myth, a word, equality is unachieveable, and fraternity means nothing whatsoever. We cannot forget our smug academics, sullying the letters after their names by teaching us that Marxism would save the world: but we have to try to see the funny side of Lenin in his glass case worshipped by the compatriots of Tolstoy and Chekhov. Political change is juggling with dynamite. The 'people' may demand it, but they usually hate it, they usually pay the highest price for it, and the next thing they squawk for is what they used to have, the golden yesterdays.

On the other hand, the people I am laughing at could be turning in their graves, looking over their bony shoulders, and saying, 'Who, me?'

Lenin and Stalin rid our over-populated world of one or two hundred million people by means of internal repression: what difference does a mere hundred million make? Russia lost another twenty million in the war. Hitler killed six million in his Holocaust, and lost a good few million in his wars. Communism in China cost uncountable lives, and Pol Pot massacred another few millions. Africa kills and starves its millions, Africa is disinclined to do less well than other continents in the killing competition. Have I left out a mass-murderer? Sorry, I know how sensitive and at once competitive you were and you are.

Ghostly voices are trying to mount a defence of sorts.

'We merit gratitude, not opprobrium and sneering laughter. Blood-letting used to be a medical treatment, health-giving, and the same applies to society, to populations, to excesses of the inhabitants of any land. We did your dirty work. We reduced populations, and gave you at least some years of peace. We did it with a minimum of fuss, whatever you may say. But you have let too many people into your world. You therefore now have to depend on nuclear armaments and new diseases to reduce the superfluity of 'human resources'. Will they do the job better than we did? Wait and see, you will probably not have to wait too long.'

This is not a joke. Hans Bernd Gisevius, a high-ranking member of the German Establishment who survived the Nazi era, wrote in his book, *To the Bitter End*, that in 1938 a powerful and fully-armed opposition to Hitler was poised and ready to do away with Nazism. The signal to attack would be France and Great Britain's refusal to trust, parley with, or give Hitler another inch. But, according to Gisevius: 'The minutes passed into hours of unutterable suspense, and then the sensational report crashed down upon our heads. The impossible had happened. Chamberlain and Daladier were flying to Munich. Our revolt was done for.'

Prime Minister Chamberlain returned to England with a piece of paper signed by Hitler. 'Peace in our time,' he informed his country-men, flapping the worthless paper in their faces. If Gisevius was right, and he was thought to be reliable by the judges at the Nuremberg Trials, Chamberlain could have stopped the Second World War. Hypothetically, supposing

Chamberlain had known about the revolt against Hitler; and he had stood firm instead of being conned; and Gisevius and his friends had succeeded in their aims, about fifty million people would have lived happily ever after instead of dying prematurely in the most disagreeable manner.

Luckily for us, Hitler's generals were fools, too. They look so grand in newsreels, in their grey uniforms and top boots, being driven in their open Mercedes Benzes. They look the part, those conquerors of continental Europe. Yet they invaded Russia. They forgot Napoleon, or thought they could do better than he had done. They took orders from a former corporal. Oh yes, believe it or not, generals and even field marshals clicked their heels and agreed to do the bidding of an ex-soldier who had only achieved almost the lowest military rank. 'Heil Hitler!' They invaded Russia and dressed their soldiers in summer uniforms, no woollies to withstand the Russian winter, only shrouds.

Hitler's relations with women were a dirty joke. Eva Braun, for example: she was the fresh-faced blonde showing her teeth and swinging her dirndl skirt in silent films of the social niceties on the balcony of Berchtesgaden. She was Hitler's companion for several years, and he married her in his bunker in the end. Had she submitted to the stimuli he is supposed to have needed in order to obtain an orgasm? Her predecessor, a young Hitler relation called Geli Raubal, apparently rebelled against her own reluctant participation in perverse practices. At a turning point in Hitler's career, Geli either shot herself, was shot by Hitler, or shot by his public relations people. She was possibly suicidal, she was certainly dangerous since she could sell her story and spoil the chance of the Nazi Party to seem to be fit to run the country, and the political fact of the matter was that she had to be silenced for ever. Hitler shot Eva Braun after marrying her – a wedding present with a difference. Perhaps he was repeating himself, and had rehearsed the act with Geli Raubal. Arguably, those women paid a hell of a price for letting Hitler have his way with them: death for close contact with his excreta.

Black humour has always had a heyday with Hitler's sexuality or lack thereof. We sang about it as we marched to fight him and his armies. A hypothetical linkage of Ernst Roehm, Chief of Hitler's storm troops, with Geli and Eva, is smile-worthy. Roehm looked like a beast and was not so nice as the beast he looked like. But he and his storm troopers had their uses, they beat up anyone who opposed the Nazi Party by thought, word or deed. Hitler wrote to him: '. . . I feel moved, my dear Ernst Roehm, to thank you for the lasting services you have rendered the National Socialist Movement . . . I wish to assure you of how grateful I am to destiny that I may call such men as yourself my friends . . .

In cordial friendship and grateful appreciation, I remain, Yours, Adolf Hitler.' Hitler then had Roehm shot. The shooting on 30 June 1934 followed shortly after the thank-you letter.

These are quotes from a correspondence between Unity Mitford, daughter of Lord Redesdale, and respectively her sisters Diana and Nancy. The first is dated 1 July 1934, a Sunday, and was written in Munich. 'The excitement here over the Roehm affair is terrific ... There is a rumour that Roehm killed himself ... I am so *terribly* sorry for the Fuhrer – you know Roehm was his oldest comrade and friend. Poor Hitler.' The second one included this sentence: 'Poor sweet Fuhrer, he's having such a *dreadful* time.'

Oh well, the sweet Führer was not so poor, for he got what he wanted, a great war, and he made the biggest mess and dropped it on all of us.

Jokes have their shelf-life, just as Brussels sprouts and we ourselves do. The joke of the Workers' Party, Labour Party, New Labour, Socialist Party, soft-tone Marxist Party, Communism-with-a-human-face Party, Social Democrat Party, stinks: George Orwell killed it long ago. But I wonder if I can squeeze a snigger out of the news that Tony Blair, our former Prime Minister, yes, that Tony Blair, may become the President of the European super-state. Will he be crowned? Will Europe be called Blairland? Watch out, mind your backs, remember to bow to Tony and curtsey to Cherie!

Some of us think Blair competes for the title of the worst British Prime Minister – and, incidentally, that his side-kick Brown may beat him to it. For the sake of our friends in France and other outlandish places, if they get Blair as their president, I hope their senses of humour are in good working order.

My operation, as numberless boring stories have begun ... But the story of mine may be a little less boring than some because it poses a question of considerable interest.

This is the factual part. The other day I hurt myself, my back hurt not badly but I was impatient, could not wait for it to get better – as it later on did – and made an appointment with a chiropractor. She took an x-ray of my back – she could not treat me until she had checked up on my skeleton. The following day I was rung up by my GP, who told me an irregularity in my innards had been revealed by the x-rays – I had an aneurism in my aorta – that is, in spoken English, my abdominal artery had ballooned out to a perilous extent. As a result a surgeon advised me that action was called for and an operation was much less risky than hoping the balloon would not burst. The operation is now planned and I have been lucky. The metaphysical part starts here. I never knew I had an aorta, it gave me no trouble or pain, and if I had not hurt my back, gone to that chiropractor, if she had not had x-ray equipment, if she had not recognised a medical condition that was outside her range of expertise, and if highly qualified medical personnel had not acted as they have done, I would not be less than a week away from the chance of rectification of what has been wrong with a major artery. But for all those ifs, I would be living in fairly blissful ignorance of my interior balloon that could burst at any moment and kill me.

What are the odds against my being in the position I am now in? Why should so many unlikely coincidences have occurred to bring me to where I am? Did someone say chance? Five or six things happening against the odds cannot really be explained in one word, chance. No, the fact is that I am the beneficiary, potentially the great beneficiary, of forces that are not factual, reasonable, explicable by senior wranglers or science, or in any materialistic terms.

'Destiny' sounds better than 'chance'; but destiny refers to the future not the past. 'Fate' is not a pleasant word to apply to my auto-biographical footnote. A question rather than an answer springs to mind while I ponder the mini-mystery of why I may have been spared a bloody crisis: what do athiests think about the favours of fortune, good luck and the alternative? They know all in a negative way, they are know-alls, so I must try to remember to ask one of them to share his or her knowledge with me.

Meanwhile, until the happy day when I am enlightened by the rejections and denials of atheism, I thank God for sending me along to the chiropractor and into the hands of my surgeon. For me and I trust for Gilly, dangerous ignorance has been replaced by hopes of health and vigour. Of course every medal has two sides: the anaesthetic could be bad for my brain, the tool of my trade, and I could meet my Maker, who has caught me in His net.

8

I write, therefore I am.

The above is a variation on the theme of the seventeenth-century French mathematician, scientist and philosopher, René Descartes, who wrote: *Cogito, ergo sum,* 'I think, therefore I am'. My variation is not accurate, I hope, since it suggests that I write without thinking.

I was operated on twelve weeks ago, three months. My surgeon told me I would have to spend five nights in hospital. What then, I asked, what would happen to me after the five nights? 'You will resume normal life,' he replied. The other day I heard of a woman in my situation who spoke of 'getting back to abnormality'. I have not yet got back to it. Will I ever? Was 'normal' what I used to be?

I have suffered no noticeable pain, and when feeling decidedly unwell I was often told how lucky I was.

Samuel Butler quotes from the Bible: 'I was sick and ye visited me', and concludes: 'This must have been a complaint'.

More notes for my study of *The British Philistine*: our kings and queens should not be aesthetes. Royal families take too much interest in the arts at their peril. Some monarchs build beautiful cities and palaces with golden interiors, but the people are not grateful for their good taste.

Presidents are generally in a more precarious position than royals, they lack the 'rights' conferred by birth and coronation. And they are always under suspicion, since they can get round their terms of office: for example, President Mugabe, the tyrant of Zimbabwe, who governs by brute force, is now serving his sixth term. Law-abiding democratically-elected presidents have to please their electorate as best they can. Voters are not prepared to wait for justice while their president finishes a book or goes to the opera.

The rulers of countries should try ideally to establish links with their people of all classes. Terror works, but not permanently: the terrifying secret police of the USSR, of East Germany, of the People's Republic of China, and so on, were swept away by popular uprisings without too much trouble. The facts that voters are inclined to 'float', be fickle, and turn against their governments, are best countered by means of identification to some extent with all subjects, and especially with the masses who wield most power. Top dogs remain longer at the top not by growling and biting but by obviously working hard, getting trusted, and winning affection. In other words, they have to embrace with sincerity the values of Philistia.

Members of the Establishment, the good ones, sit through functions, sporting fixtures, fund-raising dos, not by counting the minutes until they can go home, but by appreciating the efforts of the organisers and joining in the enjoyment of the audience. Constant exposure to the entertainment of the many reduces their chances of learning to love the preferences of the few.

Snobbery and inverted snobbery are the bedrocks of philistinism. For one reason you copy your social superiors, for another reason you spurn and jeer at the stuff and nonsense the toffs say they like best.

Snobbery has close connections with fear. You are afraid of being unfashionable, or you want to show the world that you are not afraid of being different from those people who think they are richer and altogether better than you are. You fear humiliation. You are ambitious, you compete, in order not to be humiliated and to be in a position to humiliate others; or you are the opposite, you glory in your lowliness, you show off by refusing to step on to the ladder to a higher class.

The rejection of the culture of the class above yours is a feature of inverted snobbishness. You would not think of listening to a famous diva whose voice was trained for many years, you would rather listen to the warblings of an untaught child, a 'natural', a pretty amateur. Are the masses of people who buy her recordings saying: 'She's good enough for us'? As she makes much more money than the professional singer, are people judging her voice by her bank balance? They read pulp fiction, go to second-rate films, hero-worship more or less wrong heroes and heroines, and choose to play safe according to the standards of where they feel they belong in the social pile.

Philistines were once sorted out by reference to their brows – foreheads, that is. People were highbrow, middle-brow, low-brow. Thus categories were created, and sheep separated from goats. Highbrows loved the art that was not understood by middle-brows and bored low-brows to death. Middle-brows loved art that the highbrows considered simplistic and the low-brows could see was not their cup of tea. The low-brows hated art but enjoyed loud music and vulgar jokes.

> Shikspur? Shikspur? Who wrote it?
>
> *High Life below Stairs*, James Townley
> (1714–1778)

Our brave new world has abolished the upper class. Political correctness has muddled everything and everybody up. 'Upper' has become a taboo word. 'Aristocracy' is altogether unspeakable. Equally the word 'lower' is never to be used, and would be banned if possible by the 'thought police'. A representative of the old working class is now 'a member of a hard-working family'. We are living amongst the bubbles of soft soap, where we are all winners, and the country groans under the burden of suspecting it is actually on the losing side.

Tony Blair said: 'Everyone wants to be middle class.' Perhaps that was better than insisting that everyone would prefer to be a 'comrade' of every other member of the 'masses'. But Tony Blair was wrong. Henry Green, the novelist, whose real name was Yorke, was told in an interview on TV: 'You're middle class'. He replied: 'I hope my mother didn't hear you say that, she has spent many years trying to teach me not to be middle-class in any respect.' Yorke/Green was an aristocrat by birth; and his answer certainly struck the interviewer, and probably most of the audience, as Double Dutch. Yet we know by means of recent scandals that men will pay millions for the title of a lord. Rich men aspire to be higher than in the middle of the social orders. Distinguished men and women yearn to win titles and medals. And writers likewise would if they could be above the middle in the scale of worth, not middle-brow, not middling, and not the entertainers of the proletariat.

Modern philistinism is drugs-for-fun, binge-drinking, 'conceptual' art, photographs posing as pictures, plagiarism, most of pop music, hyped books, critics without integrity – and I think it would be prudent to stop there.

And to switch without too much difficulty from consideration of offences against the ideals of truth and honesty to the problems of crime and criminals. Liberals are sad to see that their merciful and indulgent treatment of lawbreakers is not repaid by less crime, they wring their hands and hurry to build more prisons. Here are a few suggestions that might make our country safer for law-abiding citizens.

1   Dispose of murderers without too many exceptions, and cut the number of appeals against the sentence of death;
2   Deport foreign wrongdoers, and again cut the number of appeals against it;
3   Revive beating for less bad offences, the punishment not to be delayed, nor to be excessive, but to be publicised so widely as to shame those receiving it and their families;
4   The granting of bail to be reconsidered, also the theory of care in the community;
5   Speeding up the administration of the law, the workrate of lawyers, and reconsidering 'Legal Aid'.

Brickbats will be thrown at the paragraph above – barbaric, savage, old-fashioned, immoral, cruel, etc. But when times are harder than at present, 'draconian' law will be resorted to, will be popular, and in some form enacted. So-called 'civilised' attitudes to crime, criminals and wickedness are a luxury.

A rainy day in the meteorological sense; also in

the political and economic sense; also inasmuch as it is evidence pro and anti the theory of climate change; also in being good news for gardeners and bad news for holidaymakers; also in being exceptional in a dry spell of weather; finally, an excuse for not going out and getting wet.

'Terrible as an army with banners.' This poetic phrase, this brilliant observation, this truth applicable to all the tyrannies of the twentieth century, is a quotation from *The Song of Solomon.*

I am reminded of things I have left undone. I have not repaid in full my debts to friends, especially the friends of my writing. Robert Sheaf and Val May were the companions of my apprenticeship. I was lucky to meet them when we were all living on air and high hopes. Robert had the rare ability to support, encourage, and even inspire. Val was a dedicated seeker of the truth, whose idealism was infectious. No references to careers, which are anyway recorded elsewhere, simply thanks to friends who brought about turning points in my life.

After the publication of my first two books I found myself without a publisher. Carlo Ardito, the proprietor of St George's School of English and Foreign Languages, made two suggestions: why not set up our own publishing house, and let his business pay the costs of publishing our books? The consequence was St George's Press, which was instrumental in getting thirteen of my books into print. Carlo gave me the chance to reach out to my readers without interference.

But the partner of St George's Press, Hamish Hamilton Limited, decided unilaterally to disagree with our gentlemen's agreement. As a result St George's Press went into voluntary liquidation, and I was again at a loose end in Grub Street. Then Ben Glazebrook, owner of the old-established publishing house, Constable, became my friend in need. He published six of my books.

Ben's retirement coincided with my book *Evening*, in which I announced that it would be my last novel – *Morning* and *Evening* were meant to be the book-ends propping up my collected works. But how can writers of fiction be trusted? Anthony Trollope declared that he was 'done' in his autobiography, and then wrote fourteen more books. I met Carol Biss, managing director of The Book Guild, and she has been the moving spirit of the fourteen books I have written since *Evening* – I do not presume to compare my writings with Trollope's.

Anthony Trollope had an explanation for his astonishing output of prose: 'It's dogged as does it.'

Just as the nature of women is to tempt men, so male authors are tempted to analyse women. Men in general spend a lot of their lives trying to understand women, mothers, sisters, girlfriends, wives, mothers-in-law. Womanisers are pleased to think they do understand women; but 'getting round' is not understanding, they conquer more by caring less for women, they mislead and are misled by their conquests, and usually prefer the company of men.

I am no exception to the generalisation about male authors. I have the nerve to believe that my lifelong study of the opposite sex should not be wasted. Inhibitions, discretion, respect and tact are all very well, but the passage of time eventually gives permission to spill the beans.

Today, in the western world, womankind stands with her feet on the ground, posed fully frontally, she does not have to be imagined in the altogether, and she is saying she is changed, and other females are confirming it in strident voices. They are boasting, they are almost crowing, like cocks. They now have the pill that allows them to behave no better than men. They stand defiantly, they sit on their fortunes, the promiscuous ones, the wealthy exes, the single mothers in their council houses denied to married couples, the thoroughly modern regiment of statutory equals who used to belong to the weaker sex.

All rules governing sexual intercourse are bad. Every generation makes them and every generation breaks them. Feminism has won women a few more 'privileges', a bit more 'equality'; but it often seems to serve the base instincts of men more than the needs of women.

111

Forget the gains of women and count the losses! I would repeat that the pill weakens women's rights. How can they plead frailty when other women fight in the front line in wars? How can she ask to be made an honest woman, married and given a surname for her child, when abortion is no longer reserved for cases of extreme ill-health and hardship? How are poor girls to convince rich men that they are not going to take them to the cleaners legally? How are women to persuade boyfriends and husbands and other men they are not going to pinch their jobs? The morality and conventions of yore were tough on women; but are today's immorality and unconventional carry-on any better?

I am on the side of women, I am a lover of women; and love in my opinion is eagle-eyed, but I feel honour bound to rewrite clearly the old rules of loving for the shorter-sighted. Sex should be the end of a 'romance', not the beginning, although I know the experience can cut corners, and women are blessed or cursed with the ability to make up their minds about a member of the opposite sex even quicker than men. Remember, 'romance' is short whereas the post-consummation period can be very long: it can also be romantic without the inverted commas. What engages your love, what merits it? Well, looks catch eyes. A pleasantry, a joke, what is admirable, a touch of heroism, and a reputation for gallantry that means a partner is unlikely to be embarrassing in an intimate situation: these are the weapons that men traditionally carry into the war of the sexes. But are women warriors deep down? Do the majority of women want to express their love by fighting? I suggest that the true love potion even more potent than sympathy, is kindness: kindness, a little word with big meanings.

Think of all it deletes from the written and unwritten bonds between a man and a woman: violence, cruel treatment by the stronger party, a rule of terror, unfaithfulness, dishonesty on the personal level, excessive self-centredness, bad manners in bed, unprotective attitudes towards you and your children, hostility towards parents and family, hostility towards your friends, uncontrollable temper, quarrelsomeness, foolish-ness with money, hopelessness as a father. You may have the misfortune to be inextricably linked with someone who causes you to sigh, 'If only, I wish, what would I not give, alas, alas!' He may be virile, rich, too popular, the toast of the town; but the man of your dreams is not a kind person you can confide in, who will listen to you and be gentle and receptive, and you can trust and look up to.

We learn in our youth that men and women are made differently, and we are excited beyond measure by the difference. I speak, or write, for myself. But in time we all learn that the difference contains the seeds of error, risk, and potential tragedy. They are that men love as men do, while women start in the same way and then love as mothers do. Nature draws men and women together, and steps between them to remind women that they have the capability and the duty to reproduce the species.

Scoff as you like, modern miss! Scoff along with that other girl who refuses to be bossed about by a mere writer in his old age! But what do you and your cronies have to say about the children you forgot to abort? How are you to be a loving mother, a career girl, to act on the theory of free love, and hang on to the father of your children, all at the same time? Strike out whatever you will not be able and do not mean to do! Or does feminism tell you to make still more of a mess of things?

Love was designed to be complementary. One heterosexual in love provides services to another loving heterosexual of the opposite sex, and the consequence should or could be sexually satisfactory and 'a marriage of true minds'. But the heart can have reasons that are unreasonable and unsatisfactory. One party to a love affair can feel more complemented by the other than the other feels; and love moves mountains but will not be moved. It will not be forced, and fidelity that is unwelcome and obstinate is never a winner.

That some women want to be like men is strange and sad. They miss the point. They are potentially mothers, they may be the weaker sex but have to be the stronger one in many ways, and the civilised world – not only the Roman Catholic religion – recognises its debt. The virgin at her wedding, the mother and child, the beautiful ladies, the sorrowing victims of cruel men, they are our heroines and our icons. And the sweetest of all the pictures in the bulging book of my memories are of women, a smile, a fleeting gesture, an idiosyncratic avowal of grace and charm, not especially intimate but fraught with femininity and romance.

The first Duke of Wellington, the Iron Duke, is reported to have said: 'No woman ever loved me, never in my whole life.' The report is in W.R. Troubridge's *Introduction* to Charlotte Herrick's edition of *Wellington's Letters to Miss J.* Two interpretations of the Duke's statement are possible. He could have been offering up thanks that he had not been embroiled in a love affair, or he could have been voicing regret. The latter strikes me as the more likely. His Grace had won almost everything that is winnable – battles, a war, the gratitude of a nation, international renown, political supremacy, honours and titles galore – yet the prize of private life eluded him. At least, by my reckoning, he shows great wisdom by confessing to failure, and by his acknowledgment that love has a value over and above the valuables heaped upon his head. He proves he had imagination and sensitivity, and that if he was wistful he was not wrong.

The Greeks halved the worth of their philosophy by not thinking women were love-objects. Peoples in other lands, in other eras, worshipping other gods yesterday and today, look down on their women, and treat them accordingly. The fair sex can be more than unfair, can be prejudiced, malicious, spiteful, harsh and more vulgar than men. But the female medal has two sides: it can rise to the heights in the atmosphere that suits it best. Away from the fashionable fads, feminism, political correctness, snobbery and inverted snobbery, far away, where it can love and be loved in harmony and happily, its pretty ways, refinement, sagacity and unfailing resources of devotion command respect and gratitude.

9

Summertime, and the living is not so easy. The country is bust. We are in the middle of July and there is no sign of global warming. We are governed by politicians suffering from *folie des grandeurs*, who will confiscate all our savings. Cold weather now and cruel taxes to follow are getting us down.

The odd thing is, considering our snobbery, the ignorance of the titular expressions of our class system. An old Labour politician of some years ago, George Brown, a class warrior of the worst type, a deliberate vulgarian, was 'kicked upstairs', as they say, meaning that he was given a title and deposited in the House of Lords. Thereafter he should have been addressed as Lord Brown, but, either owing to the general ignorance or to his own contrary pride, he was widely known as Lord George Brown, proclaiming to all and sundry that he was the son of an eminent aristocrat, a duke or a marquess.

Who is Lady Euphemia Head-in-air, what is she? She could be the daughter of a duke, marquess or earl, or she could be the wife of a baron, baronet or knight, and people have insisted on interposing her first name between 'Lady' and 'Head-in-air' incorrectly. The mix-up may be typically English, and not of great importance, but it spoils the principle of the thing and nullifies the message.

The French aristocracy before the Revolution were far more pedantic about their titles, witness the half-crazy snobbery of *The Diaries of the Duc de Saint-Simon*. Now the French differentiate between pre-revolutionary titles, conferred on their families by hereditary monarchs, and the Napoleonic titles handed out by a temporary Corsican 'Emperor'.

The vocabulary linked to snobbism owes more to those 'looking up' than to those 'looking down': it is the vernacular of underdogs and inverted snobs. A 'toffee-nose' describes haughtiness; 'lording it' is self-explanatory; 'la-di-da' means pernickety, and 'hoity-toity' means arrogant; 'smell under his/her nose'; 'too proud to put his stick to the ground'; 'thinks he's God Almighty, thinks she's the Queen Bee'; 'scum' meaning both what rises to the top and what is filthy and foul; the cockney joke, 'Eton and brought up'; 'a madam'; 'pillocks'.

I am not a snob. I believe I am not snobbish. How can I be so sure? When I was young I was eager to know real writers. I thought the world of their books and of them, irrespective of their personalities and characters, so I suppose I should plead guilty to having been an art-snob. If ambition, aspiration, idealism and even hope are taken into consideration, also admiration of role models, an awful lot of us are unintentional snobs. We are fearful of doing less well than we want to do, and of loss of status and 'face'; on the positive side we have faith in a better happier world full of better people and places out of our reach.

Read the words of my heroes on the subject of their aims. According to Goethe: 'Nothing is great but the true, and the smallest aspect of the true is great.' Tolstoy wrote: 'The hero of my tale – whom I love with all the power of my soul, whom I have loved to portray in all his beauty, who has been, is and will be beautiful – is Truth.' Isaiah Berlin wrote about the powerful critic Vissarion Belinsky: 'Belinsky believed that the purer the artistic impulse, the more purely artistic the work, the clearer and profounder the truth revealed.' They and their peers all praise what is true and recommend the pursuit of truth in beguiling language. But the truth is a mystery. It is a will-o'-the-wisp, a moving target, indescribable, a very personal matter, even though the generations recognise and respect a truthfulness that suits their cultures. Moralists, otherwise known as artists, are truth-snobs.

And they put faith first. My literary heroes are

no less heroic because I am older and more sparing of worship. Goethe was not claiming that he knew more about truth than others and had actually found it. Tolstoy was not telling us his writing was true, truer than anyone else's. Belinsky never claimed that he was the truest critic that ever lived. May I presume to correct great writers? They were, they always are searching for truth; and they have faith that the truth is worth searching for.

People say they have no faith, they have lost their faith, they ask what faith is, they do not hold with faith, and they could never have faith in any religion or philosophy founded on what is unseen, unknown, unlikely, and a package of outdated superstitions. The Bible tells us that the man who said 'There is no God' is a fool. What do I have to say? I would point out that the person who has no faith in anything is dead or as good as dead: does he or she not have faith that 'his' heart will beat or that 'he' will be able to take the next breath? Has 'he' never lived for love or hate or anything? Has 'he' no interest in where the rainbow ends?

God is not dead, it is the man who said He was that died.

Fools who bother to proclaim that God is dead, who deny that God ever lived, are the contrarians, the inverted snobs who are nonetheless snobbish, the anti-religionists. People who never bother their heads with religion, and do not marry, let alone in church, or christen their children, or take any part in religious practice, are like political 'don't-knows': the intellectual variety call themselves agnostics. How do such people react to crises, danger, sorrows, sentences of death, pandemics, wars worldwide or civil, tyranny and despotism? I suspect they seek shelter and safety in the Houses of God. History corroborates the idea that when all else fails they have to have faith in one Almighty or another. It is only a small step between having none and having some: faith is what has been helping to keep you alive from your birthday onwards.

Faith is one thing, religion is a whole lot of other things, practised in a particular building, with others, at set times. And religions get involved in controversy and politics. Although their founders may be god-like, and lay claims to divinity in their life-times, the religions that celebrate their teachings are man-made. They seek to be the intermediaries between their gods and their congregations, but churches are subject to the characters of men, the frailties and the whims, the passions and the errors. The same applies to the pious who attend church services, their souls reach up to heaven while their bodies are earthbound. Even if some of us prefer to approach God privately, we belong to a gregarious species and cluster and cling together for reassurance and protection – in church, probably. Our religion is reinforced by

121

our co-religionists; but faith is or is meant to be an exclusive relationships between each of us and our god.

That is, between us and a mystery. Faith would not be faith if it was not belief in what was impenetrably mysterious. Faith is beyond knowledge, reason, science. Religious faith is the greatest of the expressions of the human imagination, is, was and will be, yet is a nothing, an idea that is hard to explain, the arbiter of history, and our fate. The multi-millions of our ancestors thought it was perilous to disbelieve in God. The multi-millions have worshipped and pleaded with and thanked God. Look at the shrines built worldwide to honour God! But He has different faces. He is unpredictable, and cannot be bought. We can only communicate with him by means of faith.

Is faith self-hypnosis? Is it delusion? Does it matter? A nurse I was privileged to know had unshakeable faith in her god. She asked no awkward questions, she entertained no disturbing doubts, she was a clever woman and lived successfully to a good age. My mother with her catalogue of tragic experiences never lost her faith in God, and set an example of kindness and broadmindedness. Again, a painter and philosopher for her friends told me that her religion was the basis of her lifetime of remarkable work. I could recall many other beneficiaries of the love of God, personally known to me and read about, and history has its galaxy of saints recognised and unrecognised.

I do not forget the wars of religion and pseudo-religion, the oppression in the names of God or his opposite number, the wickedness and evil. Religion is blamed by some because of its bloody record. God is in the dock for crimes committed by His children. But He in collusion with nature has equipped us with free will for better or worse. We do as we please. Blasphemy is not a crime in every country or according to all laws. We can break records for killing. God is not to be counted on to intervene or reverse our decisions. Apparently He is not moved to spare us suffering. His will has to be done. What has become of His miracles? I believe they do still happen, but slowly.

Old age is not for cissies, according to Bette Davis, a film star of long ago. Nor is life, say I! Life is a sequence of challenges, death is the last of what we should be used to. Premature death is particularly nasty because of being a surprise. Life is often referred to as the gift of God: which can be taken satirically, and regarded as a provocative statement. I prefer to think it is worth thanking for, notwithstanding life's problems and predicaments. Anyway, God has other gifts to bestow on us, which imply benevolence despite evidence to the contrary. With luck, rewards of the personal mundane type can seem to you to outweigh the sadness and the horrors of life on earth. On the level at which our race pines for religion, for a God to pray to, one of the rewards for faith is peace, inner peace, a peace as mysterious as its source, a peace too mysterious to be described in workaday language.

A lady of my acquaintance told me that, in her opinion, the most seductive sentence a man can address to a woman is: 'Leave it to me.' I hope I do not blaspheme by wondering if that is the message God has for the faithful.

10

The end of New Labour is in the tea leaves. The death throes of a political party in power are a distressing spectacle. On the other hand, we may get a government that is not ashamed and exhausted, fresh faces, brighter ideas, fewer wars, less folly.

> Knowst thou the land where the lemon trees bloom,
> Where the gold orange glows in the deep thicket's gloom,
> Where a wind ever soft from the blue heaven blows,
> And the groves are of laurel, and myrtle, and rose?

I found these four lines of poetry in my Dictionary of Quotations, Everyman, 3rd Edition, 1936, two volumes. The author was Goethe, 1749–1832, and they are a quote from *Wilhelm Meister's Apprenticeship*. The translator is not named, but there seems to be a reference to Byron. Perhaps they are famous and well-known: they should be.

When I was five or six years old, my parents had

workmen in to rebuild a summer house. I was very interested in the work, and made friends with the workmen. One of my friends said to me: 'Hold out your hand and shut your eyes, I've got a present for you.' I did so, and he touched the palm of my hand with the burning end of his cigarette. Such is life, you could say – a false friend and cruelty.

My luck was not to discover the bad side of human beings and the ruthlessness of nature too soon. I had the chance to benefit from the veil that protects children from fully recognising the consequences of cruelty (the reason why children are so good at being soldiers and shooting people). That veil is the self-centredness of youth. To suffer cruelty and understand it, that it is caused deliberately rather than by accident, is a sort of coming-of-age of the soul, a milestone on the road to growing up.

My reaction to the burn on my hand was to shout 'Ow', perhaps cry, and definitely fall out with my friend. I reacted naturally enough, but did not jump to philosophic conclusions.

We come of age in the soulful sense, if we ever do, by linking the cause and the effects of cruelty, and by imagining those effects on others. The list of people who never passed that milestone is depressingly long, the tyrants, the conquerors, the hard fathers, the unmaternal mothers, the martinets of husbands, the heartless women, and so it could go on.

You are a peace-lover, sensitive, well-meaning, good and hopeful: how are you to steer clear of the cruel people? For once a slang phrase will do for an answer: no way! You cannot elude the lunatics who want to rule the world, or the oppressors who are determined to prove a political point at all costs, or wars, not to speak of accidents and illnesses. Sadism is easy to feel, but difficult to recognise in the social setting. Other people are enigmatic, and close relationships are a toss-up. Danger dogs you, and often catches you.

The written word is not the last word. There has never been a statement that is beyond qualification: religions deny that 'death' means 'the end'. I do my best to write clearly, but second thoughts are the opposite of pats on the back. Sympathy, a favourite word, is cryptic, not crystal clear. By 'sympathy' I do not mean sentimentality, or socialism's dumbing-down to try to assist the less intelligent, or the liberals' reluctance to differentiate between good and evil, or today's taboo on the words 'crime' and 'punishment', or just friendliness and decency. My idea of sympathy is unselfishness. It is a spontaneous response to need. It has limits, defined by religion, morality, tradition and a sense of proportion. Within those limits it is generous, but not generous to a fault. It is graduated, and rises by stages to the promotion of happiness. The outgoing force of it can be protective.

Happiness is lovely, the pursuit of it is the trouble. An interest in cricket or brass-rubbings is safer than pursuing happiness via love; but sex cares nothing for safety. I have suggested that youth should read books in order to learn from authors' experiences of love, sex and the rest of it; but that suggestion requires qualification, too. Authors' love-lives seem to be rotten examples for anyone to follow. Dickens was a horrible husband; Thomas Hardy ditto; Graham Greene's sex-life was pretty disgusting; Pushkin's marriage was disastrous, and Tolstoy's deteriorated into hypocrisy; and most poets should have to wear red ribbons on their tails like kicking horses. Authors have a tendency to be or go mad. However, they are supposed to shed their eccentricities when they get down to writing; and the proof of the pudding is in the reading. At least Dickens' books are fraught with information about men. Tolstoy drew an idyllic picture of a marriage in *War and Peace*, and Pushkin's death in a duel was a cautionary tale. Hardy understood love in his writings even if he was an uncomfortable lover, and Graham Greene's work ought to scare people into looking again before they leap into the arms of Eros.

By the way, Eros was the God of love, also, in one text, a comedian.

Women have taken over the novel. They used to do embroidery and knitting. On the whole they are cleverer than men, and excel at most of the things they turn their hands to. They are bound to write from the female point of view, and about love.

The lovable and mysterious aspects of women, and their power to wreak havoc, are a good subject for stories. And men should profit from reading about the likes and dislikes of the opposite sex, and never pick the wrong girl or get entangled in the thorny shrubbery of the wrong one. But they do both. Both sexes do both, pick wrong 'uns and get entangled. For those who have not read better books by a few women, and missed the point of pulp fiction and porn, here is a list of the pros and cons of women that men should bear in mind.

There may be warning signs partly concealed in her desirability. Is she too thin or too plump, too hungry, and does she have fat relations? Are her eyes too close together, and is her bottom out of proportion compared with the rest of her physique?

Her health could become a worry. She should not be ailing. She should not be mad about medication, take drugs secretly or for fun, have a weakness for doctors. Is there a fault in her genes – or jeans?

She should not be fitter than you are, a fitness freak, hyperactive, a frenetic player of outdoor games, who even cheats in order to beat you at ping-pong.

She should not be noticeably intellectual – no pudding-basin haircuts, no drabby clothes or blue stockings. Is she able to do *The Times* crossword puzzle before breakfast, and does she boast about it? A big brain is as dicey as an excess of brawn.

Does she embarrass you with her bad manners or the loudness of her laughter? Does she put you off with some of her behaviour in the bedroom? Have you had to learn the lesson that a coarse woman is coarser than a coarse man?

Is she truthful? Have you caught her flirting with another man as she flirted with you to start with? Is she a spendthrift? Does she support herself financially, can she, could she?

If your answers to these questions are yes when they should be no, and vice versa, and my remarks make you uneasy, pause! Pause, please, and think again!

The pros, unlike the cons, will fit into a single sentence: the object of a man's love is an angel from heaven and he is determined to be her proud possessor, husband, lover, other half, servant, slave, if humanly possible and come what may.

And he may be right. But if he is wrong he has surprises in store. Each of the sexes can be equally awful in their different ways. Beyond that sort of female awfulness, nagging, shrewishness, sluttishness, they have the power of weakness on their side. They can be raped, they have the excuse of the accessibility of their genitals, and, given the chance, they can do a lot of damage to men who have forced issues between their legs. They can hit below the belt by casting aspersions on a partner's endowment, on his prowess, and sneer at his performance, draw odious comparisons that make him jealous, and spoil his pleasure by interrupting his climax or yawning at the critical moment. His confidence can be so undermined as to reduce him to impotence, and then he will have to pay the price of failure. A sex-starved woman is the loosest of cannons. Spinsters who do not become fine people turn into viragos, living on grievance.

The laws of this land now favour women. He will be accused of raping her rather than the other way round. She is more likely to get hold of his money in a divorce settlement. Most of the injustice of 'love' is done behind closed doors. In private, angels from heaven can look suspiciously like vipers. Count the casualties! There is Tom, whose wife spent his money, He is now working overtime to earn enough to pay her alimony. There is Dick, whose ex-wife makes it as difficult as possible for him to see his children. And there is old Harry, who escaped the complaints of his wife by taking refuge in dementia.

Last night on TV we had an atheist preaching a sermon about godlessness. He was like a missionary spreading the glad tidings that religions are trash and we should believe in Charles Darwin who discovered evolution. I switched off and perhaps missed the point of his disillusioning discourse to schoolgirls, who might have been hoping for an after-life. Atheists are always telling us we were created by the Big Bang or by evolution from primeval slime, but they do not know who made the Big Bang or got the primeval slime going any more than the rest of us do. They are grim puritans who would strip religions of their mystery, beauty and encouragement.

I diverge. And I cannot apologise for not sticking to the point. Old authors are tired of telling their stories without diverging. I hope I have earned the right to ramble; and the death of A.I. Solzhenitsyn is the best of reasons to do so.

Solzhenitsyn was a great literary genius and a great hero. He wrote great books, *One day in the life of Ivan Denisovich*, *The First Circle*, and above all *The Gulag Archipelago*, and he wrote them under the direct threat of extreme punishment by the USSR. They are not love stories in the personal sense, and, since I read them in translation, I cannot comment on the style of the writing except to praise its cutting edge. These three books amount to several thousand pages and innumerable words, an output of unflagging excellence, more than enough work to prove the greatness of the author. The theme throughout is the love of humanity and pity of the sufferings meted out by man's fellow-men. The plot is the revelation of how unjust injustice can be – law is the hero that is persecuted and tortured to death. All the writing was completed in secret, in the lethal police state created by Russian communism. Solzhenitsyn single-handedly, by means of the aforesaid books, showed yet again that the pen is mightier than the sword. He defeated the government of Russia, the USSR, the Bolsheviks, communist misrule of the empire of the USSR and in the countries behind its Iron Curtain, and Marxism as a valid instrument of politics. He brought about the demolition of the Iron Curtain, and relative liberation to a large part of the world. I admire and respect him. I remember his wondrous achievements, and the breathless thrill of reading what he had dared to write. Now the lefties in Russia and elsewhere nibble at his reputation and try to disparage him: which I consider his ultimate accolade.

Solzhenitsyn died aged eighty-nine. He had been in the Gulag, where life was worse than nasty, brutal and short, had had cancer, and diced with death at the hands of communism's secret police, so eighty-nine years was a ripe old age. Pushkin died aged thirty-seven after a life of privilege and luxury.

Here are a few relevant facts of Pushkin's life and death: born into the upper class, a published poet at fifteen, a womaniser and wastrel; exile and poverty served to develop his gifts, but fame made him feel he was a spent force; met a sixteen-year-old society girl and became infatuated with her, eventually married her and sired four children; their marriage disastrous since she was a nitwit and dragged him deeper into debt; challenged a man to a duel for flirting with her, received a wound in the duel and died of it. His death was foreshadowed by his own account of Lensky's in *Eugene Onegin*. The poet Lensky, too, was jealous and challenged Onegin to a duel for flirting with his girl.

Solzhenitsyn and Pushkin are not so easy to relate to as my favourite English writers are. Tolstoy said he thought Russians were most like English people. I cannot agree; although I love a good deal of Tolstoy's writing, I would have been at once scared of him and dismayed by his conduct. Pushkin in his dissipated phase, and when he posed as being old and hopeless in his early thirties, would have irritated. And why did he bother to marry the opposite of a soulmate? The American writer, Olga Carlisle, gave up seven years of her life to helping Solzhenitsyn to get his books published, at the end of which period she published her own book, *Solzhenitsyn and the Secret Circle*. She reveals that the Russian writer 'had singled her out as a traitor to my country in time of war, and a destroyer of democracy' – not a nice description of the services she and her husband were convinced they had rendered.

Eminent writers seem to end their days sadly. Fame is not synonymous with happiness. Solzhenitsyn in America lived behind a security fence, in a sense he chose to imprison himself again.

The road to love is defaced by notices warning

us to wait, stop, turn back, and is partly blocked by wounded lovers returning from wherever they have been; or am I thinking of the garden path?

Women writers should have told us the whole truth and nothing but the truth about love. One or two of them have proved they are the experts in that line. Male writers are better at depicting the romantic appeal of women.

In despondent moods I fancy that everyone has sooner or later received the gift of a burn by a cigarette end. We are hurt. We are disillusioned, lonely, have been treated badly, have had no luck. We have either been bombed to smithereens or have experienced the tender mercy of Marxism, Nazism, and a variety of other isms. And sympathy is in short supply, unselfishness is rare.

Where is the land of the lemon trees?

11

Either you are alive, in which case you will go to the party, or you are dead: this is one of the laws of 'society', and there is nothing between the two options.

Poor people! Whenever politicians plan to do, are doing, or have already done dirty work, they justify themselves by claiming they are guided by 'the will of the people'. Dictators, autocrats, tyrants and despots put the blame for their bad behaviour on 'the people'. 'The people's' this or 'the people's' that is responsible for oppressing hundreds, thousands or millions of persons made of flesh and blood. Those who fall out with 'the people' are subject to dire punishment. To call a country 'the people's', or ditto the citizen of any country, can somehow mean trouble.

Catch phrases change almost as quickly as the fashions. My mother told me that when she was a girl her father pleaded with her not to say 'you know' so often. The modern equivalent would be 'at all': 'Would you like more to eat at all … Have you had enough at all?' The overture to a sentence, 'to be honest', is now so common as to be almost a nervous tic. The overworked adjectives in U-speak are 'fantastic' and 'amazing'.

It is now four months and one week since I had my operation, and normality still eludes me. No doubt my surgeon would advise me to take my age into consideration. Candid friends might say either to my face or behind my back that I have never been normal anyway. But I would say in my defence that I am not a well-known hypochondriac, do not exaggerate much, and am not keen to show strangers my scars and boast about my ordeals in hospitals. Is it high time to beg the medical profession to give their patients a clearer idea of what they are in for? Such a novel rule might not suit everyone, doctors and surgeons would have to do a little bit of discrimination whatever their egalitarian politics.

The surprise of my discovery of the snail's pace of convalescence is not reserved for myself. It turns out that my friends and acquaintances have convalesced from operations at least as slowly as I am. The villain of the piece is apparently the anaesthetic: six months, even a whole year, is the possible time-scale for shaking off the after-effects of having 'poison' pumped into us – philosophers say it is the price we pay for painlessness. Other people tell me that they too lost their short-term memories and some of their long-term ones: to forget the subject of a conversation in the middle of it can be embarrassing. Ailments visit us for one reason or another, but surely because of the upset of our nervous systems in the operating theatre. What we have to try not to forget is that the alternative to the above could well be curtains.

I am grateful, really have been lucky, and will be a patient patient in the meanwhile. My ingratitude and grumbling stem from my protective attitude to my work: granted, everybody wants to be healthy, but, rightly or wrongly, anyone with a vocation to do something gets frantic if he or she is unable to do it. It probably boils down to the terminology beloved by psychologists professional and amateur: I have obsessive tendencies, I am a closet paranoiac. But lots of other writers and artists would share my feelings.

An example of the above: the brother-in-law of an old French impressionist painter died. The wife of the painter told him that he would have to attend the funeral, it was his duty, no excuses were allowable or would be understood by her family, he must give up a day to the payment of his respects to a close and dear relation. The painter at last sighed and agreed to please his wife: he would do the decent thing. But he remarked to his friend in private: 'These women will stop at nothing, nothing, to get me out of my studio.'

An opposite type to my painter with his vocation spoke to me thus about the books he and I wrote: 'I used to be a bloody slave of my three hundred words a day. Are you still doing books? Are you still getting into print? Oh well! Take my advice, old boy! I wrote a couple of serious books, literary novels – how? – with difficulty – and had a struggle to get them published, and my receipts were zilch, not enough money to feed the cat. But I saw the light and switched to soft porn. Result, wealth, health and a happy-go-lucky lifestyle. I can tear off a book in a month, I do four a year, otherwise it's holidays – South of France in late summer, Switzerland and the skiing, then England for the flat racing and Scotland for the grouse. My wife loves me for giving her a good time, my children love me for my money. Soft porn's today, art books are yesterday. Catch up, all you have to do is to take her knickers off on page two!'

That good-time-Charley did not suffer from guilt. Whether or not guilt is inspirational is a moot point, but it certainly tightens the screw of tension which produces the energy that is the be-all and end-all of creativity. Energy is what actually makes the world go round. It may also be the mother of mayhem; and it causes havoc in the guilt-ridden psyches of artists who neglect to obey the call of their destinies.

The act of creation is joy and jollity provided there are no hitches. You avoid the hitches by desire on the one hand and fear on the other. The opposite of the satisfaction of desire is wretchedness. A writer's 'block' is an instrument of torture. You are 'blocked' by loss of confidence, sense of failure, sense of futility, regrets, penitence and in the end the death-wish. Is mankind prone to something like it? All authors are. Today's philistinism, the rejection of quality by the modern publishing industry and the literary Establishment, must be 'blocking' much talent. Drink and drugs are traditionally resorted to by sufferers. I think of L.P. Hartley drinking vodka before breakfast and a lot more afterwards; and of James Stern's forty year 'block', although that might have been due to inadequacy. I think of the suspect silences of authors, sometimes unbroken, otherwise escaped from perhaps by means of a slim volume.

To write about art is supposed to be a sign that the writer is over the hill and generally done for. My supposition is that such an opinion was broadcast by a writer who was never much of an artist.

To write more is to read less. Reading was my education: I learnt valuable things at school although I forgot most of them without delay. My attention is still caught by a well-written sentence in a book, a sentence with grace and wit, and then by a story and the original inventive way it is told. I am more interested, amused, excited and uplifted by creative fiction than by factual, historical, biographical, autobiographical, and dry-as-dust academic books.

Do I hear the word, 'Heresy!' Do I hear a howl of disagreement and derision? The article of faith for today's literary bigwigs is that factual is good and fiction bad. All the little Hitlers who abolished the Retail Price Maintenance Agreement for books, all the publishers who only have eyes for sales, all the critics who never review novels in case they make an unforgivable mistake like André Gide – he advised against the publication of Proust's masterpiece – and all the sheeplike readers who follow wherever bribery and corruption lead, have ruled that the umpteenth biography of a popular figure or a journalistic report of war or scandal are of more cultural significance than a work of the imagination along the lines of Shakespeare and our great novelists. Literary novels are a stinker for profit right now. God knows what 'the people's' choice is.

Jane Austen was neither over the hill nor done for when she 'wrote about art' and stood up for the novel as follows:

'I am no novel-reader; I seldom look into novels; do not imagine that I often read novels; it is really very well for a novel.' Such is the common cant. 'And what are you reading, Miss?' 'Oh, it is only a novel!' replies the young lady, while she lays down her book with affected indifference, or momentary shame. It is only 'Cecilia', or 'Camilla', or 'Belinda': or in short, some work in which the greatest powers of the

142

mind are displayed, in which the most thorough knowledge of human nature, the happiest delineation of its varieties, the liveliest effusions of wit and humour, are conveyed to the world in the best chosen language.

Jane Austen spoke for herself. How do the rest of us approximate to her starry ideal of a novelist? To recapitulate with apologies: talent should not have to do hack-work that would teach it dangerous tricks – not to be a breadwinner is an advantage. Talent teaches itself, but landmarks along the ascetic way warn that the better the writing the less likely it is to make money. Vocation has to be very strong to stand up to today's barbaric hordes and win a nod of approval from Jane Austen in her heaven. For a last laugh, consider our literary institutions. In my own experience a book won a prize for irrelevant reasons because I and the other members of the jury were over-ridden by one juror; the Arts Council awarded a bursary to a wealthy writer; the Royal Society of Literature failed to attempt to protect writers from the harm of abolition of the Retail Price Agreement.

Many years ago I was instrumental in offering the British Library a donation of twenty-seven long letters written by Marcel Proust – it had only three at the time. The donor was the secretary of the late Violet Schiff, I had agreed to act for 'Miss Almond', as Violet and Violet's circle of friends called her although she was married and had children. The BL accepted the offer with alacrity, and the curators I dealt with agreed to Miss Almond's only condition, that she could meet George Painter, Proust's biographer who worked at the British Library. In due course I handed over the letters, and the BL again promised to arrange the meeting with George Painter. That promise was broken. 'Miss Almond' only received a printed form of thanks for the donation. Many more years elapsed and I offered to bequeath my archive, manuscripts and letters, to the BL: it was accepted with alacrity. The Chief Executive of the BL, Brian Lang, and the Curator of Modern Literary MSS, Sally Brown, were both 'delighted' by my prospective bequest. That was in 1995. In 2008 the Head of Western MSS, Dr Scot McKendick, rejected the bequest and reneged on all BL's 'promises' to me. How would you describe such behaviour? Anyway, my mistake, my mistakes, were to imagine that the BL was above suspicion, staffed by lovers of books and literature, unworldly idealists and proud guardians of historic high art. Not so! The British Library is just another bureaucracy, neither more nor less trustworthy than the Whitehall politicians. A few good curators exist and are not simply Civil – and occasionally un-civil – Servants.

Thirteen years after the BL disagreed with what it had agreed to, and six days after informing me of the U-turn, the offer to bequeath my archive to the East Sussex Record Office was accepted with appreciation, gratitude and every sign of professionalism on one side and satisfaction in the permanence of the arrangement on the other. I am the more satisfied as the copyright of all my books will be inherited by the Department of Cardiology, Royal Sussex County Hospital in Brighton. I regret my involvement in the con trick played on Violet's secretary — not by George Painter, I am sure he never knew that false promises were made in his name by some low librarian. The Schiff letters from Marcel Proust were always extremely valuable, they belonged to Miss Almond, who donated them with great generosity, faithfully carrying out her employer's instruction, and acting with integrity and honour, unlike the British Library.

Considering the amount of trial and error, of trial and tribulation, that go into the writing of anything good, I am mystified by the authors who stop writing soon after starting. Pierre Choderlos de Laclos (1741–1803) wrote only *Les Liaisons Dangereuses*. He was a soldier, he became a general: does that explain it? His father was ennobled: did he ask his son not to shame him by writing another scandalous book? *Les Liaisons* is a horrible story very well told. It must have been satisfactory to write, and its public success must have somehow pleased the author. How did he avoid the addictive effect of authorship? Another French example of an interrupted literary career is even more mysterious. Arthur Rimbaud

(1854–1891) was a famous poet at seventeen and said goodbye to literature at round about twenty-one – the times of his life are as equivocal as the rest of it. He went to do trade in Africa and died at thirty-five.

But now I have a confession to make. My accentuation of the negatives of the pursuit of art, my forebodings, and urgings in the direction of caution and consideration of other careers, are part of the writer's story. But I may have misled by not explaining why, if a writer's lot is so hard, costly and usually unrewarding, I have stuck with it for sixty years and am still doing so. Materialists would have reason to call me crazy. Common sense would have to agree. I think the time has come for me to try to explain what is 'on the other hand'.

In short, there are rewards. Once, to have written a sentence that worked and was not going to embarrass me was the sort of change that is like a holiday. After so many sentences, I still get a kick from trying to write a good one. To shape a chapter and plot a book are treats otherwise reserved for the gods. To live in a world you yourself have imagined is the most agreeable form of escapism. Your characters become your best friends, and no one can kick you or do you down. You are the ruler of the secret kingdom of your creation. And its weather is yours to command, its sun revolves round you, and the moon waxes and wanes as you please. You summon storms by means of a few words you have scribbled, great rollers crash on to beaches, and the sea is stilled, and your people make love in the dunes on sunny afternoons. You are in charge of their happiness and sadness, and their emotions are your own.

Is that clear?

12

This country's contradictions and illogic seem to be gaining ground, and nature has apparently chosen to add to the confusion. Our summer has been wintry, and we have been colder than ever thanks to global warming. No cuckoos round here, and the swallows and swifts have decided to stay away.

'Labour' is a misnomer. It stands for less labour for more money. New Labour looks more and more like old Labour. The Labour Party used to speak up for the working class, and no doubt it righted wrongs, but the extra money it obtained for the workers enabled those workers to climb the social ladder, into the middle class, the *bourgeoisie*, and look down on their former classmates.

Sneer not at my comments on the class system! I was born into a grand old family, but I am a second son, therefore a commoner, have had experience of snakes as well as ladders, and kept an open mind. I can claim with some confidence that I know the classes of my compatriots better than Karl Marx knew his 'masses': the revolutions he inspired were just another unintended consequence.

So-called 'Labour' governments have always made me uneasy. They smell of the politics of envy, and are ready and willing to wage utopian class wars. Democracy is probably the best of the various forms of government, but 'best' does not mean ideal.

My ancestors were the New Rich once upon a time. In the seventeenth century a Fane married an heiress, his son married another, the family was not far from the top of the world, and spent their money, nearly all of it, between then and now. 'Breeding' can work well, look at racehorses, but most people are not bred with as much study and attention as racehorses. A man or a woman is 'well-bred', to generalise, because he or she has been reared on money. Money, and not only manners, maketh man. Poor people can also be distinguished, but polish and shine will be bought with gold.

Ignorance likes to think an 'English gentleman' is somehow above money. Highfalutin personages believe it is not gentlemanly to talk about money in society, and caddish to boast about your own; but men retain their seats at the top table by often thinking of nothing else and doing their level best not to lose it.

Ignoramuses think the USA is such a pleasant

country because it is classless, unlike England. Tell that to the Vanderbilts! Tell it to the residents of New York who were not included in the '400'! The difference between society in America and in England is that in the former the aristocrats are multimillionaires whereas in the latter they are sometimes hard-up titled folk.

'Old' is not an unqualified compliment paid to a family. In hamlets and villages old families were more or less inbred because in days gone by travel was difficult. Does that account for the village idiots? Wealthy old families are also apt to be inbred because 'high society' was a limited and exclusive caste of the well-heeled, and cousins married in order to preserve their wealth. English men went to America to kill two birds with one stone, to find 'new blood' to freshen up their families and new money at the same time. English fortune-hunters were a feature of American social life at one period, and the mothers of the rich American girls would say to one another, 'Remember, trust funds only!' They were warning against giving money to sons-in-law to squander and waste, and advising retention of control over any gift of money by wrapping it in a legal straitjacket.

Transatlantic marriages were a toss-up then. The Americans had not heard the rumours about English families, and vice versa. Perhaps everybody is better informed nowadays. But men marry girls from foreign lands, girls marry men they find on the internet, parents have no advice to offer children about blind dates, and there are many undesirable consequences.

I am so old that my memories are social history. My father was a naval officer, he made a career in the navy because his parents had him educated at Dartmouth, but was thrown out of the service by the politicians' economy drive after the 1914 war. His career in Civvy Street was to be a gentleman jockey, a racehorse trainer, an amateur golfer of note, and, strange to relate, a popular lord invited on to the Board of Arsenal football club and to every sort of sporting function and occasion. His predecessor in that line was Lord Lonsdale, the 'yellow earl', so-called because his cars were painted bright yellow and possibly his racing 'colours' included that colour. They, Lord Lonsdale and Lord Westmorland, my father, were surely the last of the pop aristos and the first of the celebs. My father was recalled into the navy in the Second World War, but his health was not equal to the job, he was again returned to Civvy Street and to Dad's Army. He died relatively young, aged fifty-five, when I was twenty-one. I did not know him well, I never saw much of him what with school and the army, and to my great regret I never asked him the thousand questions I would now love to have answers to.

My father was not literary, but he met and made friends with writers, as he made friends with the rest of the world; neither was his father nor his grandfather literary. About four generations of my family were not bookish – and I am not a 'Fane' in that respect. And those forefathers of mine were poor businessmen; my grandfather had to sell the family home in Northamptonshire, Apethorpe Hall, and nearly all its contents. But later in my life I discovered that a namesake of mine in the Victorian era had been a poet and translator of poetry, and his son, Julian Grenfell, was another poet, and one that I admired. Later still, in 2001, I was surprised to receive a heavy beautifully produced book of the poetry written in the seventeenth century by Mildmay, 2nd Earl of Westmorland. I believe he and I created a record by belonging to the same family and being prolific authors across a gap of four hundred years.

My mother's father, Lord Ribblesdale, immortalised in the Sargent portrait, looked romantic, dressed in a romantic style, was nicknamed 'the ancestor' in England, and in France '*ce grand diable de Milord Anglais*'. He married a daughter of Sir Charles Tennant, ace Scottish businessman, and they had five children, two sons who died gallantly in wars, three daughters. The family name was Lister, the family home was in Yorkshire. They were not so 'county' as Fanes, more sophisticated and amusing, and more brainy, although my great grandfather on the Lister side had been as bankrupt as my Fane grandfather.

The Ribblesdale title died out with my grandfather, who had outlived his two male heirs. The present

Earl of Westmorland has a daughter, no son, and the heir presumptive of the title is his younger brother. Primogeniture, the English system that entitles the eldest son to inherit his parents' property, works better for wealthy people than dividing the spoils and passing on titles to all the children.

Two of the daughters of Sir Charles Tennant, rich but not aristocratic girls in their teens, were allowed to entertain young men in their bedroom. That was in the late 1800s. In the 1930s an aristocratic girl of my acquaintance was not allowed to go to London shops without a female chaperone. Nowadays an unmarried teenage girl and her boyfriend can sleep together in their parents' homes – unmarried older couples do. No statistics available; but 'free love', widely preached and practised, makes for no more happiness than the sexual disciplines of the Victorians.

The vocabulary of love is notoriously changeable. Rachel Cecil in her novel *Theresa's Choice* writes about dancing partners at a ball strolling into the garden 'to make love'. She had not caught up with the fact that 'to make love' had become synonymous with copulation. Today's vernacular has been dragged through the dirt of wars, barrackrooms, and the inverted snobbery of socialism: to talk broad is the done thing for pseudo-intellectuals, fashionable females and cocky males – they have robbed our language of its innocence. As for the patronising encouragement of regional accents by the BBC and the educational establishment, it has fouled up the tuition of reading, writing and spelling of English, and the understanding of it at home and abroad.

Drugs are not what they used to be. My Fane grandmother had an addictive personality and died young, and my father, her son, inherited it. He drank and smoked more than was good for him, tried without success to control his passion for alcohol, and was unaware of any reason to break his smoking habit. The anti-smoking lobby had not got busy in my youth, almost everybody smoked, non-smokers and teetotallers were regarded with suspicion: a father advised his daughter, 'I couldn't stand a son-in-law who didn't drink or smoke.' Chain-smokers were common. I knew several, one carried a box of a hundred Player's cigarettes in the pocket of his jacket. I remember a man who had worked in the Far East and wrapped up the tobacco he smoked in his pipe, he would wrap it in one of those papers used for rolling your own cigarettes, place the small parcel on the bowl of the pipe and light it – looking back, he was obviously copying the manner in which opium is smoked and he had probably smoked it.

The paraphernalia of smokers has become a footnote to social history. Cigarettes were sold cheaply, five in an open-ended mini-pack. The

Americans stuck to paper packets when we used cardboard. Pipe tobacco was sold like wines, endless varieties for different prices. Cigars were a class item – the most expensive had to be rolled on the thighs of Cuban girls. Spitting-tobacco was a cake. Pocket cigarette cases ranged from tin ones at Woolworths to bejewelled ones from Cartier. Fabergé in Russia made big ones for Russian cigarettes, and when he had fled the Russian revolution he worked for Cartier making *objets d'art*, including cases of luxurious design and wonderful enamelling fit to be kept in a lady's purse. Cigarette lighters were another full range of class items. Table cigarette boxes were offered round along with cigars at smart dinner parties, while fags were proffered in pubs, at work, all over the place, just as pipes of peace were smoked by and with Red Indians. My brother and I smoked in our childhood and studied and imitated the gestures of the smoking adults. The news that the craze for it was bad for you was countered by encouraging rumours: a twenty-a-day man had lived to be a hundred, and tribal people in the back of beyond lived to be a hundred and fifty on a diet of apricots and home-grown cigs. We smoked for pleasure, for our nerves, we inhaled to be manly and prove our strength, and we kept the secret that we sometimes felt faint after a strong cigarette or a cigar.

I can claim to know alcoholics inside out – not a boast, a rueful admission. I have gained the knowledge by unwelcome experience and by observation over many years. The symptoms of alcoholism are fairly well known but the duplicity and guilt take people by surprise. The obsessiveness is under-estimated. I offer polite sympathy to people with hangovers and *delirium tremens*, but I have become a closet prude and in my heart I am not very sympathetic. The middle-class topers used to be criticised for getting 'as drunk as a lord', the lower-class boozers for drinking the housekeeping money and starving wives and children. The passage of time has added former ladies to the list of alcies and a growing number of naughty girls who cannot wait to get into trouble.

I wonder why people yearn to be drugged by pills or hypodermic injections, and dread the side-effects of my own medication: am I peculiar or a coward? I confess I am scared by people who have chosen to be under those mind-bending drugs. And I am depressed by naïve halfwits who continue to claim that usage of cannabis is harmless, and by a government which has ruled that pubs can stay open for twenty-four hours a day.

Nothing changes. Sometimes I fancy that our forefathers clothed in animal skins and crouching in caves worried about the weather, and where the next meal was coming from, envied and despised the people in the cave next door, were tied in knots by social etiquette, were anxious hosts and hostesses, and despaired of their children.

157

But surely we have progressed a little further than our savage ancestors, I can bear witness to a difference between life in England sixty years ago and now. I refer to procreation, sex, and the finer feelings that direct men and women to the bedroom. The pill and abortion almost on demand have eased life for adults; but if they are the swings, there is also a roundabout. I was brought up to respect women and to marvel at their favours. The idea of manhandling a girl hardly crossed my mind – prostitutes might be another matter. My friends felt as I did, we were all virginal whatever the virgins were. The relationships of boys and girls in other classes were equally restrained if not more so – engagements could last years, meetings were often rationed by circumstances, girls were usually subject to curfews, and upstairs was out of bounds. The result was romance, yearnings, the stuff of poetry, a test of compatibility and fidelity. All that has gone west. Is that a good thing? The thrill of a hand held, a little kiss, and those sweet illusions have to be compared with sex for certain, your place or mine, a pill to be remembered, and with luck a wedding in undeserved white on one fine day. Perhaps we missed chances and wasted time, and today's preoccupation with sex at once, no holds barred, is the new 'puritanism' notwithstanding the lack of purity.

My childhood could be called idyllic: I made a sort of idyll out of it in my first book. We lived in the west country, a farm was across fields, the nearest house inhabited by strangers was a mile away. Our home was sheltered by trees, they formed a wind-break for the grown-ups, we children climbed them and made rickety houses in their branches. I remember mostly loving faces, the man who burned me with his cigarette was an exception to the rule, and the dentist was a friend despite his drill. The weather was never bad in my recollections, it was either fine out of doors or gave a chance to do carpentry and stuff indoors.

We were five siblings. Our differences did not seem to stop us having fun. We were allowed to be free, we enjoyed a freedom that would horrify the Health and Safety brigade. Anyway, we came to no harm.

Our parents had private cares and political anxieties. Unselfishly they did not allow shadows to be cast over our years of ignorance. It was a good time for lucky children. But the gulags were being created and the ovens being lit. Here's hoping the twenty-first century will be better than the twentieth.

13

I am not superstitious, my wife was born on a thirteenth day.

The world was revolted and ashamed by the homicidal chapters in the history of the twentieth century. Then dictators in the East took leaves out of the book that recorded the offences of Bolsheviks and Nazis. We grew accustomed to shocking news. Time inures to almost everything. Comparisons were a negative kind of comfort. The nineteenth century suffered Napoleon. The eighteenth century witnessed the sacrifice of native populations. No century was humane. We are the most bloodthirsty of all the species. We are also the most successful, we over-populate the planet, instinct advises us to reduce our numbers by slaughter if nature has not done it by disease. Realism is another philosophy.

I would like to be philosophical, it would become my age. But I think of the lady in her eighties who was asked, 'Is it a relief to have achieved the peace of the senses?' She replied to her young questioner: 'My dear, you will have to ask somebody older than me.' The title of this book does not suggest that the contents are deep philosophy; and would a novelist write an astrological study, or go in for astronomy and foretelling the future in his eighties? But *The Night Sky*, the three words and the physical phenomenon, have a lot of meanings and mysterious charm, and seem to me to be relevant.

Politically we wait. We sit at the bedside of New Labour, waiting for its departure. How much longer is our vigil to last?

David Cecil includes a quote from *The Diary of a Nobody* by George and Weedon Grossmith in his *Personal Anthology, Library Looking Glass*. It comes in a section named *Humour*. It is wonderfully funny. In *A Reader's Encyclopaedia*, first published by Adam and Charles Black in 1965, *The Diary of a Nobody* is not included. It is a classic and is ignored. There is a snobbery in the literary world about jokes: they are despised. My sister June, one of the most humorous of women, surprised me by claiming in her later life that she had never laughed at a book: was that a joke? The Germans were supposed by English people to be lacking in the humour department – lacking that, too. In a film about the war an actor playing the part of Goering was shown sitting at his desk and reading an issue of *Punch*. He looked hard and without smiling at page after page and demanded of his aides standing at attention: 'Is this funny? What is the joke? I am not amused.' But we laughed at the scene.

*   *   *

Opera is becoming more popular in England, it is winning a new audience. Excerpts from operas are the accompaniment of TV adverts for cars, toothpaste, food etc; there was a competition on TV for amateur opera singers; pop groups succeed by singing jazzed-up operatic arias; the word 'pop' is tacked on to the word 'opera' in various ways. Pretty girls who can sing a bit make big careers, comedians make hits by mangling opera in their music hall turns, children make fortunes by chirping *Ave Maria*. Their 'ratings' are high, public opinion polls call the girl who has never had a singing lesson 'the greatest diva ever', while the male vocalist is rated 'better than Caruso'. Money proves it all to 'the people': these performers of opera-based 'easy' music, almost musak, are showered with gold. We hear of them moving their millions off-shore to avoid tax, getting into long legal arguments with the Inland Revenue, quarrelling with international music companies over their contracts and because they have sacked their 'managers'. Meanwhile, persons gifted with voices and aspirations to sing the operatic repertoire are being trained to do so, a lengthy and rigorous process. The 'trainer' should be qualified at least by experience; a young voice should be held back until physical development gives it the requisite strength; temptations to sing too soon for money have to be resisted; funding until the age of possibly the mid-twenties of a female singer will be an all-round strain. And the future of the more professional singers is not rosy for all: jobs scarce, recording engagements thin on the ground, pay mingy, work when available exhausting, success reserved for few. Art is difficult and dangerous, and the Philistines are always ready to pose and posture and pinch the limelight from artists.

Some of us do not look upon youths, the noisy ones, the violent ones, kindly. But there is one young man I respect and admire. Read on, all will be revealed! Auctioneers send us catalogues of pictures they hope to sell. A smaller part of these catalogues show 'old master' works of art, a larger part shows 'modern' art, from Picasso onwards. As a rule I like a few of the latter examples, hate a few more, and am astonished by the estimates of prices. There are 'exhibits' amongst the pictures for sale, a tray with butts of cigarettes on it, dead flies in a glass case – is anyone going to pay through the nose for them? What are they doing in a sale of works of art? They are curios, to put it politely. Other items, although painted, do not deserve to be sold by an auction house with pretensions of expertise and good taste: I am dogmatic because I know I could cover a canvas with paint, nothing but paint, no pictorial element, and that artisans could do it better than me. Then I jump to a critical conclusion as I dump yet another catalogue in the WPB. Picasso's artistic legacy has been awful. He was clever to make so much money, his wealth persuaded the success-snobs that he was right to distort human physiology in his pictures; he gave a blessing to the untalented practitioners who could not draw and had no message for mankind. Andy Warhol followed in his footsteps: he made a killing in photography, his 'pictures' that sell for millions are snapshots. Well, the boy I would congratulate is the hero of Hans Anderson's story, *The Emperor's New Clothes*. He alone saw and said that the Emperor was actually naked, courtiers and establishment types had been wrong to persuade the Emperor and the common people that his new suit was the most beautiful. Hans Anderson's spokesperson today would no doubt have something to say about the high prices charged and apparently paid for low art.

'Running' jokes used to amuse us. A joke that ran was to put the word 'short' before the words 'story' or 'book', thus creating a satirical conjunction. Here is an example: *The Short History of Scottish Charities*. Here is another: *Have Fun with Stalin, a short guide to the Game for Children*. I am reminded of the 'shortest' ghost story, recounted in doggerel by a man who spent the night in an old-fashioned house, had a bedside candle instead of a lamp, and woke in the dark: 'I reached out my hand for the matches, the matches were put in my hand.'

Down Memory Lane I was reminded of two books Charles Snow, C.P. Snow the novelist, urged me to buy and study, *The Varieties of*

Human Physique by W.H. Sheldon and W.B. Tucker, and *The Varieties of Temperament* by W.H. Sheldon. Charles said they were invaluable sources of information about the appearance, character, appetites, tastes and general psychology of the people who featured in his books. He thought they might be good for my work. I read them with interest, but never used them. One of the books stated that Conan Doyle had made a mistake in his description of Sherlock Holmes. Holmes was described as being tall and slender, therefore he would have been sick after smoking pipes of the strongest tobacco throughout a night.

When does education stop? More to the point perhaps, when does it begin?

I learnt something at school, one thing anyway, how to make and use my little grey cells. It was an expensive lesson. My amateurish qualifications for trying to be a professional writer were intuition and an open mind – I wrote my fingers to the bone by the light of nature. Fifty books on, and sixty years later, the lessons get harder. Reputation is fickle. You are up against the strain of struggling not to be obsolete. The literary scene has changed, moved on, but not in a direction that favours you. You are a survivor maybe, but lonely.

Winston Churchill told another truth when he said the middle of a book is the most difficult part to write. I am past the middle of this book, and the end of my books can be especially stressful. 'On the other hand' as the best Marx was apt to say, Groucho Marx: this book is not like my others, it is not like other books, which is either good news or bad news.

Pigeon-holing books is one of the unattractive traits of the commercial book trade. The publisher of my first book was torn in half by not knowing if it was an autobiography or a novel: it was the latter. There should be a pigeon-hole in bookshops for works of the imagination; but publishers could not be trusted to separate sheep from goats, and booksellers would not like to have to think of anything except sales. The phrase 'downhill all the way' in a negative sense applies to the book trade in the last half century. Books seem to have become old hat. Text messages may be the new improved English language. I am sad that English poetry and fine prose could soon be numbered amongst the beautiful lost arts of the history of civilisations. Yet, after all, all the solitary striving and the negotiations with awkward middlemen, I have finally recognised what is not my business and I do not need to mind. Old age has redeeming features; and when health allows, it can face up to common sense. My good luck as a writer is to have got so much of my writing into print, a fairly durable substance. I should not ask for more. Besides, I have three more titles awaiting publication by contract.

Politics intrude as usual. People who are not

interested in politics, read no newspaper, watch no TV and do not listen to the radio, probably spare themselves a lot of worry and woe, but I doubt it. Life is worrying, and worriers do not need politics to worry. And what would we hate without them? They tell our fortunes, entertain, scare us, they are habit-forming, even addictive, and unavoidable in the end.

Prime Minister Gordon Brown has spent my money and yours. It is going, going and almost gone. At first he scattered it about in order to make us love him, to buy popularity, and help him to win the next General Election. But now bust has followed boom, recession gets a grip of the world, and Brown borrows to stop the rot. He borrows to ward off slump but also to create difficulties for the winner of the next election. He has borrowed tens of millions, tens of billions, more money than the country will be able to repay, and certainly enough to ruin the government or his successor. Unfortunately for us, and possibly for him, largesse, money for jam, handouts galore, begin to please the people, and the opinion polls suggest that he might win the next election after all. In that case he would have to try to clear up the mess he is making.

What do the Trades Union brothers and comrades have to say for themselves in a recession? We remember when they busted great industries, car manufacturing, coalmining, the docks in Liverpool and London and, counterproductively, succeeding in getting the employees sacked. Those glory days are over. Their threats are no longer effective when everyone is threatened by somebody or something. The brothers must be having another think about bankrolling the Labour Party and paying the salaries of their 'barons'.

The slump is terrible, but I would not, could not, write about all the suffering – too many armchair messiahs are at it. The government's reaction smacks of Labour's gift for mismanagement. My country was ruined before the global financial catastrophe struck. 'The people's' choice of leaders was bad, democracy had shown its shortcomings, and now our rulers are simply not up to their jobs. Decadence lurks round the corner. Hell's bells! For goodness sake, be more careful how you vote! That is my advice, and the last of it.

A spider spun a web outside an upstairs window, it was a very large web relative to the smallness of the spider. It was made of connected circles of silk, many approximate circles spun with professional accuracy, and the spider 'sat' in the middle for several days, motionless. He or she was yellowish in colour. The web was invisible to the human eye until the sun shone and revealed the silver and gold of its extraordinary texture and architecture, the fairy-like threads, and the spider's achievement. The purpose of the web was to catch flies for the spider to eat, but not much was caught while I was watching. The idea crossed my mind that the spider was resting after its labours, and quietly approving of the result. One night the wind blew it all away and there was no sign of the spider. Such is life, and especially the life of the artist.

Cloudy September days, no sunsets, floods up north – could be worse. In my childhood home in the west country our sitting-room faced south, but through another window we could see the sun setting in winter. It set behind the trees in the grove: in summer and autumn the leaves got in the way, we could only see a radiance of various colours over the rooks' nests in the high beeches. The early dusks and the darkness of wintry afternoons were compensated for by the light and brightness filtering through branches and twigs. Shepherds' delight, red sunsets in skies clinging to the blue, were dramatic. Rooks flapped to their roosts, and sometimes great flocks of starlings did their aerobatics without ever colliding. After the sun ceased to glare and sank out of sight, nature seemed to take a deep breath and relax, like a performer when the curtain falls.

In my childhood, in bed and alone, I listened to the sounds of the creatures out in the gloaming. The white doves burbled in their dovecote. A fox might bark drily, that bark would frighten its potential dinners and at the same thrill its hunters. The hoot of the brown owl was another mixed blessing, blood-curdling and romantic. Swallows and swifts spent their summers in our country in those days, and some round about my home. They swooped and dived to catch their diet of flies even in the dark, flying to find food for their young, and shrieking as if with excitement.

The drive uphill to my childhood home had trees and vegetation on either side. The surface of the drive was rutted, puddles formed in the ruts and holes when it rained, and if snow fell they were hidden and risky. We children dared one another to walk down the drive in the night, in the dark, and I cannot remember anyone accepting the challenge. We were not cowards, we thought with reason that strange men could easily lurk in the thick undergrowth, an escaped criminal or a hungry carnivore from a zoo.

We were told that to see the crescent moon through glass is bad luck. When we heard that the moon was in its first phase and visible, we rushed to open windows and look up, or, if we were not already in bed, to run downstairs and out of doors. Sometimes the little moon seemed to sail majestically through cloud, we did not realise that it was the other way round. Sometimes we were disappointed because the moon hid behind clouds. In a clear sky the curved moon resembled a kind of cutlass. Stars twinkled at us: how and why did they do that? Nights without wind were still, the world was so still and silent you could have heard a pin drop, and the sky was high and incredibly deep.

I never believed there was a man in the moon, or that it was made of green cheese although it looked a bit like it. I made repeated resolutions to study astronomy, but kept none of them. The secrets of sun and moon, the stars and the universe appealed to me, and I was happy to think God was behind it all, without imagining that there was an old man with a white beard sitting on a cloud in heaven. And I grew up to feel more or less the same: I embraced the mystery, and my religion evolved from feelings.

I am not ashamed to be so unscientific and even irrational. My books are about life, not science. My faith is sheltered because I ask no unanswerable questions. Thanks be to science, for rendering existence easier for some of us: the good you have done outweighs the bad, I expect. But we all have our limitations. When night falls I look at the sky with wonder and ignorance. The stars I can sometimes see are innumerable, but many more twinkle elsewhere, and the elsewhere is incomprehensibly big. Science may get a prize for trying to unravel the mystery of where we are and how we got here; but its efforts seem pitiful as well as presumptive as day yields to night. The dark is a reminder of how little we are, and know. Primeval slime is squalid compared with the Garden of Eden; and who created the slime, anyway?

Night offers compensation for being impenetrable and hazardous. Love mounts its throne as the lights are extinguished; and nocturnal hunters of the human kind are in a minority. Busy mothers and fathers, employers and employees, surgeons and commuters, are relieved to rest in the horizontal, and cooperate with their transportation into the land of Nod. Cities and villages filled with sleeping people look sweetly meek and defenceless under the soaring moon and the universe reaching into infinity.

Down with the modern cult of ugliness! The point of all religions is their promise of life after death. Resurrection has been the aspiration above all else of every age everywhere. It offers the beautiful prospect of a second chance to be happy. Atheism's denial of resurrection makes death into a dead end, pointless and hopeless. Atheists know they are right, they believe they can prove they are. I would suggest that they go out at night, into the darkness when the stars are visible. They should study the stars with and without the aid of a telescope, and modestly acknowledge that they know nothing. They and science between them know the tiniest fraction of knowledge of the celestial system. Why should their guess be more right than religions'? I have sought beauty in my life's work, and I opt for the guess that is not cruel and ugly.

Again the night sky peeps through the uncurtained window of our bedroom. The dark does not frighten me any more. I have even got round to enjoying the lengthening nights of autumn and the beginning of winter, although the reversal of the process from the twenty-first of December until the twenty-first of June is more loveable: spring is such a seductive season. Sometimes I see only blackness, but by the light of the moon the clouds chase each other for my entertainment, and gales blow the clouds faster. And every so often in a waning moon I do seem to see a man lolling back on a long chair, tired out by his month of appearances.

One night, or maybe day, I may become a fragment of myself, the electric next-to-nothing of my soul, beckoned by sunshine or the twinkle of stars to be in the secretive vastness of sky. I have no objection to such a future, and quite like the idea.